ARTHUR PARKINSON

THE **FLOWER YARD** IN **CONTAINERS & POTS**

CREATING PARADISE SEASON BY SEASON

To John James Mackie

RIZZOLI
NEW YORK

Contents

INTRODUCTION

This book is an adoration of the plants that I grow and therefore know well. Many of these I have always had an instant attraction to, but others I have grown to love and appreciate more recently.

These are the plants that I want the seed packets or cuttings of, that flourish in pots. I crave them each year and plan my garden around their seasonal orchestras; according to when they need attention or are to be sown, require pruning or are to be protected against the winter cold, hankering for when they are going to be in full flower or at the peak of their seasonal interest. Each has its time to shine as the others bow out like actors on a stage, although, as gardener director, I make it all go to my personal script. Though perhaps of late, this is no longer so much the case. It really depends on the overall view that they are forming between the pots, it's as if truly they are speaking and ping-ponging off one another. Often what I find is best is to just take a relaxed view once the efforts of the spring and early summer sowing and planting are over. The trick, increasingly, is to just let everything grow and get on with it in their own time, all a tumble, a success, a death, and at times a marvelous riot.

I don't think anyone can now claim that it is possible to write a definitive garden manual, as climate change has made weather conditions too volatile and it's impossible to know what each season will hold. It's increasingly something of a guessing game. I grew up, some thirty years ago, recognizing the appropriateness of the *Bambi* song "Little April Shower," but it doesn't hold much meaning for children now as April, in England at least, is proving to be such a dry month. The climate is changing and so are our interlinked gardens. This book isn't, therefore, so much a guide for growing but highlights the plants that I have found will grow well in pots, those that have attributes of clout and glamour, traits that—especially in small gardens—are really needed when space is at a premium.

Lists, I think, are useful, as I realized after going to a garden center with my younger brother, Lyndon. New to gardening in pots, he very innocently almost bought a load of tender houseplants, and it dawned on me that offering similarly inexperienced people a book that could in part be used as a plant shopping list might be helpful in saving them time and money. After just a few years of being a gardener, though, you'll inevitably start growing your own little Noah's-Ark-like list of plant loves.

When plants engulf a garden's space, no matter how small it might be, they will, through what are now rapidly becoming confused seasons, ensure a garden that will provoke our senses with color and scent and that will welcome in the magic that is the presence of bees, songbirds, and butterflies, ethereal beings that need so much help now to survive. I hope this book introduces, or reintroduces, you to some of my favorite floral personalities and that these will become some of your cherished favorites, too. While birds are quite a challenge to photograph, this book deliberately has as many photos of bees that I could manage to snap. The extinction of all our pollinating insects is a real risk today due to the continuing use of harmful pesticides and herbicides and the disappearance of wildflowers. As individual gardeners, we can quickly take up organic gardening habits while governments continue to take the slow lane in introducing meaningful changes in law to properly protect biodiversity. Our gardens can still brim with color and also be full of wildlife-friendly plants.

PREVIOUS Summer flowers all in pots and a stone raised bed. Left to right, cosmos 'Rubenza,' viper's bugloss, *Tagetes patula* 'Konstance' (center), cardoon, buddleia mint, and echinops.

OPPOSITE Tulips 'Copper Image,' 'Ballerina,' 'Black Hero,' and 'Veronique Sanson.' Here the different heights of short and tall tulip varieties work especially well together thanks to the presence of the wallflower 'Fire King.' The clown-like 'Flaming Parrot' and smoke-pink 'La Belle Époque' tulips are in separate pots to the right.

The new flower yard

A small garden rarely has the benefit of a surrounding landscape or views, so usually you rely on plants to block out unsightly visions that close suburbia entails. A good plant skeleton is vital, therefore, if you're to have year-round interest and screening—I'm referring to the blight of dustbins and neighbors' cars or the neighbors themselves, plant all of these things out of sight if need be!

This is a more diverse and different take from when I first began gardening, to my first flower yard in fact, where every pot was planted with just tulip bulbs each autumn after taking out the summer annuals in haste, meaning that the garden was a very unstable, flash-in-the-pan creation, as well as being expensive and needy. To treat a garden like this is not only hugely demanding, it's also, arguably, not sustainable. Just one type, one group of plants making up the garden's entirety, is an unnatural monoculture too reminiscent of the often sterile Victorian bedding displays, the opposite of what a healthy, biodiverse garden should be, which occurs by having a large array of curated plants, reminiscent of the traditional mixed cottage garden.

More and more, it's important to me for the garden to have some good bones, provided by woody stems that in turn create canopies that give shelter to garden birds and other wildlife; decay and self-seeding are welcome now. Bees make me smile and feel worthy of being on this planet more than anything else, particularly when I see them being nourished within a welcoming flower that I have grown. Watching bees is an antidepressant visual, you take in the life of that bee buzzing and think, yes, I'm part of this big wheel of creation now, it's my job to look after the bees by growing flowers for them. This gives us the most honest purpose for being on this planet, which is very nurturing for your soul to feel.

By ensuring plant diversity, a plant tapestry forms and this finds its own magical and invigorating rhythm of growth. Admittedly, most of my largest pots are still designated for annual glamour, which is the spring bulb display replaced with flowering summer and autumn annuals, because the injection of these is exciting and creates drama. But the garden is no longer just an annual display in its entirety. Instead, other pots that swell around these firework-like pots contain more constant, perennial appearances to ensure there is continual form and interest.

PREVIOUS Late summer abundance, the fizz of grasses and saucer faces of flowers.

OPPOSITE An erupting rosette of silver-blue cardoon foliage. Thanks to a 2 liter (3½ pint) cardoon plant being planted on top of tulip bulbs back in the autumn, the cardoon now gives clout and fullness to the spring tulip display of toffee-orange 'Brown Sugar' and Tudor-red 'Palmyra.' The pots standing off the ground on the plant stand contain freshly planted dahlia tubers as it is now mid-spring and the risk of hard frosts is usually behind us.

MY FLOWER YARD CHARACTERS

This is a list of my favorite characters for my pots and why I love them, but please note I can grow these because my garden gets a good amount of sun. If you are in a shady situation, you won't be able to grow everything that's listed here; instead, see page 186 for some suggestions for a more shaded flower yard.

Canopies and climbers

* Plant for shelter, shade, scale, fruit and blossom, autumn color, concealment and privacy, and to encourage pollinators and garden birds.
* Small trees and shrubs include figs, crab apples, eucalyptus, holly, roses, hawthorn tree 'Prunifolia.'
* Climbers include ivy, *Hydrangea petiolaris*, passionflowers, honeysuckles, climbing roses, star jasmine, pyracantha.
* Annuals include runner beans and pumpkins.

Structure and form

* Plant for scale and effect, autumn color, winter interest, clout, glamour, harvest, privacy, and garden birds.
* To create a rib cage and a backbone of constant form through the year plant cardoons and artichokes, yew and bay, cornus, ferns, rosemary, sage, lavender and hardy herbs, kales and chards.
* For billowing and moving clumps and seedheads plant *Panicum* 'Frosted Explosion,' *Chasmanthium latifolium*, fennel, salvias, agapanthus.

Floral guests

* Plant for glamour, color, craziness, harvests, and to encourage pollinators.
* In winter plant violas and spring bulbs such as tulips, narcissi, alliums.
* In summer plant dahlias, sunflowers, cosmos, tagetes, lilies, gladioli, alstroemeria, honesty, amaryllis, viper's bugloss.

Scents

* Plant for the senses, herbal teas, and pollinators.
* Try hyacinths, narcissi, honeysuckles, roses, all herbs, lemon verbena, scented-leaf pelargoniums.

PREVIOUS The shed can be hidden with massed pots from late spring to late summer, most effective in the latter season thanks to salvia 'Ember's Wish' and dahlia 'Black Jack' (right).

OPPOSITE *Clockwise from top left* Mixing annual plants to ensure an exciting pop and billow is essential if hanging baskets are not to look uptight and dumpy. If space is truly at a premium, then hanging baskets will prove to be a major part of the garden's display. The hardy fuchsia 'Dying Embers.' As young plants these are growing in a trio of terracotta pots in dappled shade, lined up along a wall like elegantly draping exclamation marks. I'm increasingly discovering the beauty of flowering shrubs and many are especially suited to being in pots. Hyacinths are much underrated bulbs being very perennial, rich in perfume, and fantastic cut flowers. An excellent pairing of flowers in a pot according to their heights: viola 'Tiger Eye Red' provides heart beneath the airy *Narcissus poeticus* (pheasant's eye). They were planted in the same pot in early autumn, the violas flowering before and after the narcissi have finished flowering.

The power of pots

"Pots, that's real mental health," says my neighbor, Charlotte. She loves her pots despite having a big garden because, as she puts it, the work is instantly done, either by emptying and replanting, or by preening the existing plants and containers; it's instant gratification. I suppose I could portray my pots as being that, as they have certainly witnessed enough of it.

The actual magic of pots is that, regardless of what you might have in them, you can move them, you can even completely rearrange the display as if it's a posh garden center's entrance foyer, if you want to. You can't do that with an herbaceous border, or if you do start digging it up it's often a year's wait before you can see whether your meddling has paid off. With pots, though, the result and satisfied feeling of having achieved something can be immediate, and that is probably why I like gardening this way the most.

UNDERSTANDING POTS

Every pot needs to have at least one hole at its base to allow for drainage—there are no exceptions to this rule, apart from container ponds, obviously! Drainage holes need to be covered over with one large bit of crock or slate completely to stop them from getting blocked up by compost that will cause a clog. Then scatter over the top of the covered drainage holes more generous pieces of polystyrene or broken terracotta and slate. Then cover these big bits with a layer of at least 2.5cm (1 inch) of grit or small gravel. This ensures good drainage by making sure the drainage holes don't become clogged with soil and by slowing drainage, which allows the pot to absorb more water. In the case of galvanized pots, it's a good idea to totally cover the bottom with broken-up polystyrene, because this helps prevent rusting.

Always fill up pots properly, even big ones unless there is a concern over their weight, such as on balconies. There was once a popular habit of filling up pots halfway with the gubbins of old plastic or terracotta pots and polystyrene to scrimp on the amount of compost required to fill them, but this isn't beneficial to the plants. You want the bulk of your pots to be full of compost so that the roots of your plants can grow as deep as they wish. This also helps to prevent your pots being blown over, especially tall ones, which can happen if all the weight of the compost is toward the top.

OPPOSITE In small gardens a table will often be the garden's central heart. Use it as a stage, gathering pots around and on it.

ABOVE Every single pot must have drainage holes and these must be covered over with drainage materials. Without this, hopes of successful growth and plant health are trashed.

Bigger is always better. The deeper and wider a pot is, the cooler and deeper the roots can grow, and the larger a pot is, the more soil and moisture it can hold. This will reduce plant stress, too, which can occur quickly in small pots of hungry plants. Larger pots are also more impactful for a small space and are easier to manage, requiring less-frequent watering because they dry out more slowly.

If you inherit pots and don't like them, don't live with them—give them away. You can easily get too potty in a small garden and that can ruin the look, as well as make things stressful, with too many containers full of this and that, all needing attention, getting pot-bound and being eaten by various pests. Frequent sorting out and rearranging through the year is very beneficial for a little garden and your mind. A good fettle about is a great tonic.

❧ HOW TO LAY OUT YOUR POTS

Envisage your pots creating flower beds by grouping them. Only the largest or most ornate of pots can hold court as grand single islands in the middle of a garden, on a hard surface, or within flower beds. Grouping small pots on garden tables gives a collective splendor, and this position is also useful for growing things from seed and tubers, since getting them off the ground protects the vulnerable massively from slugs.

* Lining pots down either side of a garden path from a door or to a gate, or either side of steps works well, as you are treating them as if they are making flower beds collectively.

* For making doorway statements, choose pots as pairs, and go as large as you can afford or have room for. Dinky does not make a doorway look grand. Matching pairs of pots also look great on either side of permanent garden features such as benches.

* A huge island of pots can often look very lavish and imposing, and can be created by encircling lower pots around an especially large one—imagine the pots are forming tiers as on a wedding cake.

* Crowd pots into corners for them to radiate outward, the largest and tallest toward the back and the smaller toward the front, in a triangle shape.

OPPOSITE Especially large and commanding pots such as this old copper one often look their most superb if they aren't crowded out by others.

🌱 POT SIZES

The following is a list of the pots I use in my garden. Vintage galvanized metal is usually thicker and more long lasting than newly made, thin sided zinc containers.

OVAL TIN BATH

59cm (23 inches) long, 46cm (18 inches) wide at the center, 25cm (10 inches) deep
Suitable for bulb lasagnas (see page 90) of two layers, violas, wallflowers, and all herbs. Honesty, cosmos, pelargoniums, salvias, borage, linaria, *Cerinthe major*, geums, *Panicum capillare* 'Sparkling Fountain,' and *Chasmanthium latifolium*.

CATTLE TROUGH

127cm (50 inches) long, 46cm (18 inches) wide, 40cm (16 inches) deep
Suitable for salvias and all herbs, lavenders, cardoons and artichokes, cornus, bay, bulb lasagnas of 2–3 layers, lilies, cosmos, hawthorn and bird-attractive hedges, figs, pelargoniums.

OLD DOLLY TUB

48cm (19 inches) deep, 43cm (17 inches) wide

OLD DUSTBIN

61cm (24 inches) deep, 48cm (19 inches) wide
Both dustbin and dolly tub are suitable for wigwams of sweet peas, pumpkins, runner beans, cosmos, dahlias, figs, roses with accompanying salvias, three-layered bulb lasagnas, sunflowers, and lilies.

OLD COAL HOUSE BUCKET

30cm (12 inches) deep, 30cm (12 inches) wide
Suitable for pelargoniums, tagetes, linaria, and single layers of bulbs.

SMALL VINTAGE TERRACOTTAS

9cm (3½ inches) deep, 9cm (3½ inches) wide to 13cm (5 inches) deep, 13cm (5 inches) wide
Suitable for cuttings and small spring bulbs.

VINTAGE VICTORIAN TERRACOTTAS (KNOWN AS SANKEY POTS)

A minimum of 20cm (8 inches) deep, 23cm (9 inches) wide
Suitable for statement single pots for plants such as pelargoniums or treating single tulip bulbs as Dutch still-life studies. Also snowdrops, muscari, and hyacinths.

REUSABLE PLASTICS

* Sets of root trainers for sweet peas, 32 cells.

* 2–3 liter (3½–5 pint) pots suitable for dahlia tubers.

* Old square and tall rose pots suitable for lily bulbs.

* 9cm (3½ inch) square pots suitable for potting cosmos seedlings and direct sowing annual seeds into.

LARGE COPPER POT

48cm (19 inches) tall, 71cm (28 inches) wide
Suitable for bulb lasagnas and an array of summer annuals such as cosmos, tagetes, and panicum grasses.

OPPOSITE Old galvanized dustbins can still be found fairly cheaply and are on my list of favorite large pots. Here they are lined up together and have within them one of the best pollinator and pot plants, which flowers for almost the whole year, the perennial wallflower *Erysimum* 'Bowles's Mauve.' It is growing with hyacinths 'Woodstock.'

POT MATERIALS AND EXTREME WEATHER

The effects of extreme climate change are swiftly being felt around the world. This impacts plants in pots more so than those in the ground, as hard frosts and heat waves are felt more by plants in containers.

Terracotta – Terracotta is porous and will absorb moisture readily, so large terracotta pots are best lined around their inner sides with old compost bags before being filled, to help them retain moisture over the summer. I have mixed views about the need to raise large terracotta pots off the ground, as newly bought ones are usually considered to be frost-proof and none of mine are raised up on "feet." They are, though, set on graveled areas. During the winter, I place small terracotta pots on plant stands and tables rather than on the ground in any case.

Galvanized metal and metal – These absorb heat very quickly during the summer, so it's best to line the sides of cattle troughs with upright sheets of recycled polystyrene, which will help reflect the absorbing heat away from the soil and protect the plant roots. In the winter such sheets will then insulate from the cold. Round dolly tubs and dustbins can be lined with wool fleecing, the sort often used for packaging frozen food, as it has very good insulation properties.

In the winter, extremely low temperatures are likely to become more and more common. Warmer city microclimates help, but depending on the severity and what you are growing in your pots some can be protected from frost by being wrapped up with horticultural or recycled wool fleece or bubble wrap around their outsides. Mulching, which is heaping an extra layer of compost on top of the pot during the winter months, will help any plants that are considered to be tender, such as salvias, penstemons, and dahlias, if they are going to be left in their pots.

For a mulch to be successful it needs to be heaped on like a molehill or miniature flamingo mud pie nest so that its depth is a good 10cm (4 inches) at least. It can then be brushed off in late spring. You can shove pieces of broken roof slate around the rim on the inside to help mound up the mulch successfully.

OPPOSITE *Tagetes patula* 'Konstance.' Sometimes reaching 45cm (18 inches), such varieties are compact enough to not require staking but are also not dinky. These are growing in a galvanized coal bucket, having been sown back in late spring, and just one seedling quickly bushes up and fills out.

ABOVE Small terracotta pots will dry out swiftly in the summer heat, so water saucers under them will assist in them surviving, especially if you are partial to having weekends away. This one contains tagetes 'Strawberry Blonde.'

What every flower yard needs

A soft brush – To clear any hard surfaces nicely. Having a brush of the correct soft bristle so you can lightly sweep the dirt from paths without ruining self-seeding between the cracks is vital—those with goat hair are especially good. A dustpan and brush—the old metal sort that lasts a lifetime, unlike modern plastic versions— is very useful, too.

A washing line for laundry – Saves on ironing, it's good therapy, and it makes you appreciate your clothes more! Washing lines heavy in laundry require one if not several props. I deliberately coppice a good length of sturdy hazel that has a pronged V-shaped fork to hold the line in its middle. I like the old wooden pegs, but keep these nice and dry over the winter as otherwise they start to rot and the wetness of them stains your clothes!

A birdbath on the ground for birds, hedgehogs, and frogs—I use a large terracotta saucer that is shallow enough to let a frog have a cooling dip but not deep enough to allow any little birds to drown. Place a small bit of nice wood, a stump of a little log, or a rock in the middle so bees can possibly visit too. Scrub out and refresh weekly.

Gaps in your boundary – If your garden is solidly fenced all the way around, make sure there are some small gaps along the base to allow hedgehogs free access.

Comfy chairs – Not metal, these are rarely ever comfortable. Deck chairs, for me, require too much storage space for the time they can be left out in the garden without worrying about their fabric. My favorite chair is what I call the Duchess Amanda Chatsworth jelly shoe chair, which is purple Perspex, of an inward dome shape, and wonderfully comfy!

Weathered garden tables – Wonderful, always in use as plant stages and especially helpful in keeping vulnerable seedlings off the ground and safe from slugs.

Crap corner – A corner somewhere out of the main line of sight for stashing bundles of hazel, stacking out-of-use pots and newly bought plants.

A terracotta water butt – To help conserve water from building roofs, if space allows.

A cold frame – For growing and protecting annuals, see page 33.

RIGHT Sweeping hard surfaces is best done with a soft brush, especially if self-seeders are to be allowed to flourish between cracks.

OPPOSITE The washing doesn't always color coordinate, as seen here, with salvia 'Ember's Wish' and dahlia 'Bishop's Children.'

AND WHAT IT DOESN'T

What you need to be careful not to do in a small space is allow a garden shed to dominate. Never place such a thing in the middle of the garden; instead, position it to the side if possible and/or eclipse it by placing large pots in front of it that contain mostly permanent structural or densely growing evergreens, such as eucalyptus or *Trachelospermum jasminoides*. Ivy trained up metal supports, holly, yew, rosemary 'Miss Jessopp's Upright,' or bay also work well when grown in pots for constant presence. Allow wooden structures such as sheds to weather naturally rather than paint them with bold wood preservatives, although certain greens can work well as they blend into the space—this is cautionary advice after having a tomato-colored shed that was in the very center of the garden during my childhood.

Dustbins – No owner of a large garden would mention such a plague of necessity, but the number of these required for a modern household now is really quite something—usually numbering at around four, each with its own attention-seeking colored lid of red, green, or blue. If you can beg, borrow, steal, or even, maddeningly, perhaps rent space outside of the garden for them to live, then do so. At present I've been lucky with this issue; three bins and a plastic bottle box live on the outside of the back garden gates, but if you must have them within the garden, hazel hurdles that they can crèche behind will really help conceal them. As with trying to conceal garden sheds, growing ivy in metal cattle troughs with a hazel hurdle placed in the center of each, tied onto thick stakes of hazel rods, creates a good dustbin hide. The ivy will scramble up the hazel hurdles very happily, which, in fact, will be to the hurdles' advantage because the ivy clinging onto it eagerly with its suckers will hold the hurdle together even once it has become brittle; they would otherwise fall apart within a few years. You might also consider planting up such hazel hurdles with *Hydrangea petiolaris*, which, like ivy, will cling to the hurdle.

OPPOSITE The ability of seeds to self-seed into cracks and crevices is a virtue within urban environments. Here bins are foiled by viper's bugloss and caper spurge. Both of these thuggish, nectar-rich wildflowers are biennial so they will die after they have flowered, requiring them to be cut back. However by then their seeds will have fallen to germinate their next generations.

PLANTS TO AVOID

All of the following do absolutely nothing for me personally, but they are often planted in pots.

Pampas grass – Neighbors may well consider you to be a swinger if they catch sight of these, but it's also a deadly dull yet razor-sharp plant. They have it in the Gorilla Enclosure at London Zoo, bizarrely, but maybe gorillas have tougher skins than us humans. Avoid especially if you have infant children as it cuts hands to ribbons.

Phormiums and cordylines – Loved by some, and while they give structure, they do little else in a small space and nothing at all for wildlife. They drive me mad by constantly looking the same over the entire year.

Box – This now gets so many ailments beyond the fatal box blight that it's not worth the investment. Choose instead rosemary or yew for similar topiary shapes—both are better for interest and wildlife and suffer from fewer pests and diseases.

Cherry laurel – Fast to grow but its large, smooth leaf structure is of little use to birds and it is stagnant-like in its personality.

Heuchera – This is more controversial than the others as they are worthy of pots but they attract vine weevils like nothing else, so I don't have any in my garden. Apparently, though, if you add a good 5cm (2 inches) of horticultural grit as a top-dressing all around the base of the heuchera the vine weevils cannot lay their eggs into the soil, so maybe I should try them!

Euphorbia – I'm afraid this plant risks hospital if you cut it and the sap gets into your eyes, which is easily done and it's simply not worth the pain unless you garden in gloves, which, admittedly, I can't get into the habit of wearing! For acid-green foliage, grow instead the friendlier *Alchemilla mollis*.

Peonies – Another controversial one, as people love peonies. They are often the main flower that beginner gardeners ask about. You can indeed have peonies in large pots but they only flower for a few weeks in late spring, early summer (late May into June in the UK), then offer nothing for the rest of the year. You also cannot combine them with other plants as they especially resent disturbance, meaning a peony will require a large pot pretty much to itself, although they will cope in dappled shade. The only things you could plant them with to add further seasonal interest would be a scattering of delicate and perennial spring bulbs, such as snowdrops or crocus, and maybe the autumn-flowering *Cyclamen coum* around the edge of their pot. However, I have never done this myself because peonies just don't earn their space requirements for me in a small garden, I would have them in a larger one though. Peonies will not usually flower in their first year and if they are planted too deeply they may never flower—their lipstick-like buds should only be about 2.5cm (1 inch) below the soil's surface.

LEFT There are a number of budget mini greenhouses now available that offer protection to seedlings from the wind and rain. Lifting them off the ground helps to deter slugs and snails. Opening the doors or tops on sunny spring days is essential to stop seedlings from getting too hot.

WHY A COLD FRAME IS ESSENTIAL FOR SEED GROWING

I've yet to own and have space for a greenhouse, but if you have a neighbor who has a dormant one then ask to adopt it, as I have admittedly done recently. It has been a game changer as far as growing more seedlings and overwintering tender plants is concerned. This, though, has been a recent luxury, as previously I had only cold frames and modern Victorian-style glass cloches that acted as miniature greenhouses and were enough for me to grow several dozen crops of annuals through the year. What seedlings need is to be in full light, which is what these provide, but they also vitally shelter them from the wind and light frosts, which is what will kill young plants easily. All seedlings need to be out and in a cold frame within a week of being germinated inside on a windowsill. This is because it's simply too warm inside for seedlings to grow strongly indoors, and the light coming in from just one direction makes them stretch and elongate toward it within hours; the result is sickly seedlings, instead of stout and strong ones. Cold frames and miniature greenhouses should be placed somewhere that gets a fair amount of sun for at least a few hours a day rather than in the dankest corner of the garden. It is a good idea to place them on top of tables to make it harder for slugs and snails to find your young plants. Line their bases with a fabric known as capillary matting, which is highly absorbent and acts as a reservoir for water that the plants can access, which will help to stop your seed trays and pots from drying out.

If you are on a budget, a large, Perspex office storage box turned upside down and weighted with a brick on top of it will act just like an expensive cold frame. You can drill their lids to ensure water can drain from their insides. Also fairly cheaply priced are the tentlike, plastic-covered greenhouses, but these often don't last a season as they are made from flimsy materials, which also means they need to be weighted down in case of high winds, as they can easily topple over.

LEFT Old Victorian cloches will cost a huge amount but modern replicas can now be found that cost less, and lend themselves to the look of the cottage garden.

OPPOSITE Garden tables often become growing and potting benches in a small garden. In late spring and early summer seedling numbers hit their peak so it's helpful to stagger your seed sowing to prevent stress and losses. Overlooking these seedlings is the very late tulip 'James Last.'

OVERLEAF The annual summer hanging basket (page 37) has four components. Top left, *Panicum capillare* 'Sparkling Fountain,' the essential froth and fuzzy heart of many summer combinations. Top right, petunias (in this instance a typical large-flowering, supermarket-purchased variety) provide satin-like flowers. They bloom willingly if deadheaded but use scissors rather than fingers as skin sometimes reacts badly to them. Look out for the Velour Series, 'Burgundy Velour,' and 'Tidal Wave Red Velour.' Bottom right, black-eyed Susan vine, *Thunbergia alata* 'African Sunset,' and bottom left, the purple bell vine, *Rhodochiton atrosanguineus*. Both are tender as seedlings and need to be sown in late winter and kept on a warm windowsill until mild early summer.

MOLEHILL SOIL

These miniature black gold mountains offer wonderfully fertile soil, so take my advice and when you see them on public land or in a churchyard, go back later with several old compost bags and a trowel to collect the loam for your pots. I love foraging and wear an especially old, ragged coat for this so that any passersby think I am a mad tramp and therefore don't disturb me as I kneel and collect my precious soil. I didn't have to do that last year because my friend Bee had a Mr. Mole in her lawn and he was having a wonderful time providing me with lots of soil mounds to scoop up.

This most beautiful bubbled-up, mole-nosed loamy topsoil is the best thing you could mix into sterile store-bought compost mixes because it contains billions, if not trillions, of microorganisms, including earthworms that will be invaluable for your plants to flourish. So gather as much of it as you can and mix it into bought compost at a ratio of about 50:50. You will always have to mix it with compost to get the right consistency for pots. All compost you are buying should be peat-free due to the environmental impact that harvesting peat has on the planet. The current best runner in peat-free compost mixes seem to be those made by Melcourt®, whose SylvaGrow® line is used by many professional growers. Their tub and basket mix is perfect for annual displays, while John Innes No. 2 is best for herbs and perennials and the No. 4 is good for trees and roses.

I don't throw away old soil from my pots and you don't need to either, but I am constantly adding elements to spent compost that keep it alive, and molehills are vital for assisting in this. If you inherit old pots with seemingly lifeless, baked cakes of compacted compost bricks, you can still revive it. Tip the lot out and remove any old noticeable roots, fluff it all up with your hands or a garden fork to aerate its structure, then add molehill soil by a third and some fresh compost by another third. Organic seaweed meal and worm casts can be added by the trowelful, too, which are both supercharged and very high in nutrients. If you know anyone who has a compost heap, ask for a present of a bag-for-life's worth, as again this will be full of nutrients and microorganisms. It's all about treating your soil as if it's alive. Collecting deciduous autumn leaves and stuffing them into burlap bags to rot down for several months will turn them into totally organic leaf mold for free, which the following summer makes for a very fine mulch and top-dressing.

ABOVE Earthworms are essential and a sign of pots being of good soil health.

OPPOSITE Mixing molehill soil into bought compost: not an exact science at all, more of a guessing game, as you aim for a consistency similar to that of a rich chocolate cake!

COMFREY FEEDING

Comfrey, *Symphytum officinale*, is often seen in vegetable gardens, for good reason, which is because it forms a thuggish clump of hairy leaves supported by roots that grow very deeply. The flowers are loved by bees, but it's the leaves that make it a true garden asset, because they can be fermented into the best plant food for everything else in the garden (its roots also apparently produce a very good oil for the skin!). You create the feed by harvesting the leaves and stems, chopping them up, and letting them break down in a bucket of water. The result will be a very foul-smelling but nutrient-rich plant food that is especially high in potassium, making it the ideal tonic for hungry dahlias in particular. It's also an especially good liquid feed for sweet peas.

Luckily, comfrey often self-seeds, so you may be able to find feral plants growing on wasteland. I pick it over the summer because it grows along a nearby bypass, but a handsome thick clump can be cultivated in a dustbin. Once the plants are established after a year, cut the clump right down and shove all the leaves in a deep bucket of water that has a lid and leave it to brew for three weeks, by which time the coppiced clump will have already begun to resprout. Dilute a mug's worth of the comfrey tea into a filled watering can at a time; it will be a tonic to everything but realistically the fermenting of it in a small garden might be too much because of the awful smell. You can buy comfrey feed either in a liquid or pelleted form, too, although it is shockingly expensive so it's best to befriend a feral clump to harvest from!

OPPOSITE Comfrey, when allowed to flower, is rich in nectar for many species of bee and its foliage, once stewed, is a rich plant feed of potassium that will save one a fortune in not having to buy liquid plant feeds. The best variety to buy as root cuttings is thought to be 'Bocking 14.'

Almost wilding

The potential for gardens to assist wildlife is vast. In the UK, for example, gardens cover an estimated ten million acres, but that estimate probably doesn't even include gardens that are balconies or rooftops. As a nation, the United Kingdom has shamefully lost 50 percent of our biodiversity so far, resulting in us being considered one of the most nature-depleted states in the world. So every garden, no matter how small, really can make a difference if the right plants are grown and wildlife-friendly gardening styles and thought are adopted. The same is true elsewhere, of course.

I walk along streets saying "fuck off" in my head to what is now a trend of having plastic box balls and fake ivy glued to trellises, dressing entire front gardens that are completely dead and paved over for parking. It frightens me. Have our lives now become so apparently busy that we haven't even got time to prune ivy to keep it in check?

A love of bees and birds pushes me to continue gardening organically, without chemicals, to fill a garden with plants that encourage the heart-heightening excitement of seeing a visiting butterfly's fleeting presence. It's a sight more beautiful than any gem that could be purchased. But for such precious beauty to truly flourish, we must treat our gardens as gardens, rather than as extensions of the interior human domination of the house.

The famed American gardener, Bunny Mellon, was quite ahead of her time when she asked her gardeners to put the windfallen apples back under the trees as they had first found them. They had raked up the windfalls into neat little piles, but this was not to her liking because within moments the gardeners had innocently ruined what Mellon would have perhaps seen as the natural and free display of apples fallen perfectly as nature had dictated, scattered playfully throughout the grass as a natural banquet for garden birds and sugar-seeking butterflies. If left these would have also become a slowly rotting fertilizer for the parent tree itself. We need to relax more as gardeners and let it all breathe; a little decay and appreciation of seedheads are now the order of the day!

I even like dandelions now, the bumblebees' favorite! I might not want one to take pride of place, but it can get on with life if it wants to in the cracks between the bricks. If you fancy arranging something in a vase for a dinner party that will be totally free—and won't be forgotten in a hurry!—the seedheads of dandelions look incredible, especially in candlelight. You may,

PREVIOUS A painted lady butterfly visiting the allium 'Violet Beauty' (left) and a small tortoiseshell butterfly feeding from marjoram (right). The wild sort is arguably the most beautiful and will happily grow into a dense clump in a pot.

OPPOSITE My favorite way of arranging is quickly and without over-thought. This arrangement has been hugely helped by the chosen vessel, which need not be massive. This Dutch still-life style and smile-inducing array has the dandelions known to some as 'poor man's gerbera' taking center stage. Tulips include 'Parrot King,' 'Irene Parrot,' 'Veronique Sanson,' and 'Abu Hassan.' The calendula 'Sunset Buff' looks especially lovely with the dandelions—they have a teddy-bear-like character. Bedding primulas and pansies add to the tapestry here too. It is worth knowing that shop-bought flowers—frequently out of season, grown in far-flung climes and wrapped in plastic—often carry more chemicals than many supermarket vegetables, especially when it comes to roses.

though, get some odd looks gathering them from roadsides and carefully caressing them into a box to carry them home. The dandelion has about one day when it holds onto its little parachute seedheads, so you need to shake each seedhead before you pick it, to check they're not about to fall off and create clouds of fun at the dining table!

There are some wildflowers that truly flourish in a domestic habitat. The biennial viper's bugloss—which resembles a flat, hairy-leafed, dense starfish in its first year before rocketing up like a wild, electric mutant delphinium the following early summer (June in the UK)—will self-seed fascinatingly well into the crevices of a patio. The self-seeding of foxgloves (also biennial) seems not to happen in my garden as much as I would like, so autumn seedlings are planted about to help swell their numbers. Also happily tamed is the clump-forming perennial greater knapweed, which has one of the highest concentrations of nectar.

Biodiversity and the enjoyment of having animals in gardens is something that I've always found alluring. The irony of all this gardening is that it is when a garden is allowed to relax nature effortlessly flourishes with little need of interference from us. The problem is that even I wouldn't want to open my front door to tendrils of bramble and thickets of stinging nettles, and you can't really let ivy cover the windows. The most beautiful front garden I saw once was one of an almost lost lawn of tall seedling grasses with the tendrils of perennial sweet peas snaking through it. Christopher Lloyd's famous quote that the garden looks its best the year after the gardener has died is one of the best.

My garden training, though, which was not so long ago, encouraged the opposite of plant romance and dictated an overall control of hacking and tidying up of a garden, which didn't really nurture nature. I spent hours leaf blowing and clipping, tidying, even putting black dye into ponds, agonizing over my inability to create lines when mowing a formal lawn.

The great thing about having a horticultural education, though, was that I really learned how to propagate and prune properly. So if you want to help yourself and are beginning or considering some garden courses, I would recommend a few months being trained in these fields professionally, perhaps as a volunteer in a garden that grows a lot of annual flowers. You'll learn the tricks of the trade and practical growing skills that no book can properly convey.

What gardening courses can't teach, of course, is the art of imagination, which, arguably, is just as important as an understanding of plants when it

OPPOSITE The viper's bugloss is a hairy-stemmed tower of flowers especially rich in nectar, meaning that even on wet days bees will seek it out. There are more than 250 species of wild bees in Britain with many facing worrying declines. Our gardens can offer vital sanctuary to these precious and wondrous insects.

comes to planning a garden. Discovering what colors and garden styles really make you buzz with excitement is something you must find out for yourself. It might be through books, collecting images from social media and magazines, looking at designs that have been inspired by floras—William Morris is very good for this—or through watching television.

I especially love nature documentaries; I'm still inspired by one called *The Millennium Oak*—"This baby needs a good beginning if it's to last for a thousand years"—that was broadcast on December 30, 1999, when I was seven. It was narrated by Tom Baker, whose voice I'd later hear again narrating *Little Britain*! The program followed the life of an oak tree from germinating as an acorn in Saxon times, being planted by a jay, surviving being cut for firewood and flourishing having been coppiced, to it growing into a mighty tree and bearing witness to the changing world as humanity dominated into the twentieth century. The accompanying soundtrack was a perfect mix of music and birdsong, with beautiful sped-up footage of the oak growing through an English wood and the seasons. It was the first time I became aware of what coppicing is, something I now do annually when foraging silver birch and hazel for my wigwams and plant stakes.

Funnily enough, this documentary, which aired almost two decades before the notion of rewilding, made famous now by the incredible work done by Isabella Tree and Charlie Burrell on their Knepp Estate, mentioned almost all the British species now flagged as being endangered, from the purple emperor butterfly and dormouse to the nightingale.

Gardens are only wildlife-friendly if chemicals are left completely out of the domestic gardening process, and although this is something I adhere to I wouldn't say I am a very good wildlife gardener because, being primarily a gardener, I am a controller. I'm not somebody who wants complete mess, I don't own a bug hotel, and I like to brush the garden path every few days. The thing I'm learning to do more of, though, is to relax, to leave plants to fade, and to let the garden breathe as much as it can before the display of abundance is affected. It would be very hypocritical of me to claim otherwise, because in truth the most wildlife-friendly version of my garden would probably be one filled with brambles and nettles. One day, if I allow it to get to that state, I'll be that old man in the house covered in ivy who all the younger neighbors think is crazy.

Perhaps, though, that is being too harsh on myself. After all, a great number of ornamental plants that flower in our gardens when native wildflowers and blossom aren't in bloom provide a huge and valuable

OPPOSITE A hedge on a terraced street providing both privacy to the household from the sidewalk, and a sanctuary to birds. The hedge-top is a songbird nesting haven of thick and thorny pyracantha, which come the autumn will be full of nourishing berries having also provided blossom for bees in the spring. Ivy has grown and made almost a ball-gown-like understory for the hedge.

amount of nectar and pollen for pollinators. Look at the buddleia, for example. Originally from China, it's an absolute butterfly mecca and turns summer train journeys into a passing purple haze. Arguably, too, small stamp-sized spaces such as my own that are filled to the brim with wildlife-attracting ornamental plants that are tended to organically are much more valuable to pollinators than many huge gardens just composed of mowed lawns surrounded by fence panels.

I am, though, very species-specific when it comes to wildlife, I'm afraid. I'm here for the delicate and beautiful ones, namely butterflies and bees, but this is an unpopular stance now in our live-and-let-live wildlife gardening world, which has all become a bit too *Animals of Farthing Wood* for me. A fellow container-gardener friend, Philip, cannot even open his windows because the overwhelming scent of fox piss flows in from his little garden. Everything's dug up, it's absolute carnage out there. I'm not here for fox or magpie conservation!

The most important thing any gardener can do is to ban poisons! I don't use any chemicals of any sort. In fact, I'd like to write a book one day called *Fuck Glyphosate*, which is an herbicide that research increasingly shows has done so much harm to our planet, to ourselves, and to our bees and wildlife. The companies that make it have so much power that people have been afraid to speak out. It is a very dark corner that the horticultural industry has been partnered in. Glyphosate, sold as various over-the-counter weed killers, has now been scientifically linked to cancer in a number of species, us included. It kills the beneficial microorganisms not just in soil but in our stomachs too, because it's very much present in nonorganic fruits and vegetables and so gets into the human food chain. I remember being told I'd never get a job as a gardener if I didn't pay to get what was known as a spraying license, which enables you to wear a white protective overall and have a spray kit on your back. You might have seen people attired in this way, making their way up and down sidewalks, and a day later you'll see the little dandelions growing in the cracks are yellow and dying. I just knew I didn't want to be involved in that sort of work, it felt wrong and, indeed, it most certainly is.

ABOVE Buddleia, adept at self-seeding into crevices, make for perfect, easy-care pot plants and they are beloved by butterflies. Those of the Buzz Series and also 'Hot Raspberry,' as seen here, are compact and will flower for several months if they are deadheaded. In large pots the traditional 'Black Knight' and 'Royal Red' will grow into airy fountains each summer, having been pruned back to more than halfway in the spring.

OPPOSITE A flower bed lined by marjoram and the creeping tendrils of the honeysuckle 'Graham Thomas,' a hugely bee- and moth-attractive pairing planted by Becky Crowley at Chatsworth House.

A LOVE FOR BEES AND BUTTERFLIES

Being in tune with bees as a gardener is essential. I am not a beekeeper; I doubt I ever will be because it's a highly devoted vocation to be an apiarist. Our role as gardeners is to provide pesticide-free, and therefore safe, nectar and pollen for all bees, be they honeybees or one of the many, many species of wild ones.

Bees pollinate more than 75 percent of food crops grown worldwide, and collectively all bees and other pollinators are responsible for pollinating 80 percent of Earth's flowering plants. For honeybees, their resistance to the modern world—one that is now full of pesticides and herbicides, and finds them often intensively managed and fed on an unvaried diet of monoculture crops such as rapeseed flowers—has seen their adult working life spans halve compared to fifty years ago. Today, a honeybee's average life span has fallen from thirty-four days to just eighteen, and one in ten species of wild bumblebees is threatened with extinction. Globally, insect populations are seeing a decline of some 2 percent per year. It is an understandable presumption to think that bees need more beekeepers but this is false; what all bees need are more safe and diverse flowers to feed from. In terms of finding ethically produced, genuine honey, seek out a local artisan beekeeper in your area, and always have some good honey at home. It's the best thing for colds and sore throats, a truly magical gift from the bees to us.

Sometimes when you are walking along a road, or after a wet and windy day, you might rescue a bee from the ground that seems almost lifeless. It may well be dying, but it is still worth attempting a revival by mixing a teaspoon's worth of water with sugar at a ratio of 50:50. You can carefully nudge a bee onto a piece of card or tissue to lift it without risk of being stung—which will only occur if the bee feels it is being manhandled and therefore threatened. If the bee is simply exhausted rather than in fact dying, its little, black, straw-like tongue, known as the proboscis, will sense the sugar water and, although sluggish, it will try to sip the liquid from the spoon if it is placed close to the bee. Once the bee seems livelier, set it either on an open flower or somewhere sheltered in the garden from where it can fly off when it's ready to.

The root of all evil when it comes to the decline of the bee is the use of chemical pesticides. Nectar and pollen that contain chemical traces affect the entire colony. Gardens full of a diverse variety of chemical-free flowers can help hugely, as can areas of lawn allowed to flower; the dandelion is one of the bumblebees' favorite flowers.

PREVIOUS Dense hedges of mature hawthorn are as precious in towns as they are in the countryside for creating rich and vital wildlife corridors. This alleyway, shown in both winter (left) and spring (right), is constantly alive with birds and at night the grunting scuffles of hedgehogs can be heard too. The reality is that such habitats can, within hours, be thoughtlessly cut down to be replaced with sterile fences. These public spaces need local support as their fate often lies with the actions of local government that have been guilty of being too fond of brusque hedge cutting and indiscriminately using herbicides without thought.

OPPOSITE The rich, pollinator-welcoming face of a sunflower. This variety is 'Valentine,' a wonderful size of bloom perfect for cutting. Sunflowers provide large landing pads for both bees and butterflies.

CLOCKWISE FROM TOP LEFT Pollen- and nectar-rich flowers. Hellebores flowering in late winter provide both glamour and bee forage. *Cerinthe major* (aptly known as honeywort) will often willingly self-seed once introduced to a garden. Dahlia 'Bishop of Auckland' will flower into late autumn. Honeysuckles, such as this variety 'Graham Thomas,' do well in pots scrambling up fences and through hedges, too. Freshly opened flowers, such as the incredible flower of *Angelica gigas*, will be visited constantly by pollinators. All wallflowers are especially good for bees as they carry a rich fragrance in the case of annual varieties. Salvia 'Love and Wishes' being visited by a honeybee. As they flower on new growth buddleias should be pruned back, reducing them to less than half their original height, each spring. This variety is the buddleia 'Black Knight.' All herbs, like this marjoram, are wonderful bee forage. The flowers of brambles are especially popular with many wild bees and without bees visiting them there will be no blackberries to pick later in the year. Ivy, often scorned, is nature's natural way of providing for pollinators in late autumn.

The intense summer heat wave of 2022 saw my garden, like many across England, fall silent during the day, with no sound of bees, as it was simply too hot for them to fly. Then, when the heat relaxed, the bees emerged sluggishly and ill, as if they were on a harsh comedown. It was an alarming thing to witness. Bees do collect nectar banks in their hives, and so they have reserves to feed on that last them for a few days, but in the future it is predicted that heat waves may be more long-lasting and more frequent, meaning that bee populations could really struggle.

With climate change, it is feared that several commonly known bumblebees will become extinct around the world, including in much of the UK, if the planet warms by a further 2°C (35°F), because it will simply become too hot during the summer for them to be able to fly and properly forage. Professor Dave Goulson, one of the best experts and voices trying to save insects at large, aptly described their plight in the face of climate change by telling people to imagine themselves trying to flap their arms two hundred times per second while wearing a fur coat on a hot day!

The yearly patterns of butterflies and moths are incredibly diverse, owing to each species having its own life cycle. Already, half of British butterflies

ABOVE, LEFT A red admiral butterfly sunbathes on a cardoon leaf.

ABOVE, RIGHT All thistles are especially rich in nectar and cardoons are in fact one of the largest thistles.

have been listed as endangered. Some are migratory summer visitors, such as painted ladies, while the majority enter a dormant phase over the winter as either eggs, caterpillars or pupa cocoons, or indeed as adults that will seek hibernation-like refuges in garden sheds, the thick undergrowth of ivy, and within hedges. Red admirals, small tortoiseshells, commas, brimstones, and peacock butterflies will all do this.

Sometimes such butterflies will choose to settle in the unheated rooms of unoccupied houses or outbuildings in the late autumn only to be woken up prematurely by the turning on of central heating when their human occupants return. If you find butterflies in such places and it is still winter, the best thing to do is to carefully catch them up into a small cardboard box and place it somewhere that is sheltered but cold, such as a garden shed. Always try to avoid contact with a butterfly's wings, because they are covered in tiny scales that the gentlest human touch can instantly damage. With sleepy butterflies, the best thing to do if they are fluttering against a glass window indoors is to get them to cling onto a piece of card, via which they can be carefully carried into a box and be moved to a shed. Remember to let them out of the box after a few days so they can settle down to continue their slumbers. Then, on a sunny day in the spring, leave the shed door open to allow them to escape.

While warm summers may be of benefit for adult courting butterflies and daytime flying moths such as the fairylike hummingbird hawk-moth, periods of prolonged drought will often see a number of common caterpillar host plants fade out before their caterpillars have had time to grow and pupate. Each stage of a butterfly's life cycle has to be completed for them to exist in their entirety, from egg to caterpillar to pupa to indeed butterfly. Nettles, for example, a primary breeding plant for several of our most beloved butterfly species, quickly frazzled throughout large areas of the UK in 2022 and only revived once the rain returned, but caterpillars need to constantly be eating on fresh leaves; they can't pause and wait for foliage to revive once it dries up.

Prolonged wet and cold unseasonal weather can be equally problematic as it means that butterflies cannot forage easily. Climate change is therefore making it very much a yearly game of snakes and ladders for several species of butterfly. Having gardens populated with chemical-free, nectar-rich flowers and a bit of mess and decay in their corners will provide our pollinators with at least some chance of survival in an increasingly hostile and uncertain world.

ABOVE Iconic for its tall and airy style, *Verbena bonariensis* will often self-sow willingly if a sunny garden is to its liking. This is a virtue as it looks at its best en masse and all pollinators—especially the hummingbird hawk-moth—adore it. It seems to dislike being cut back until, if possible, mid-spring where new growth sprouts from the base of old stems. Over the winter the seedheads will prove popular to goldfinches.

🌿 A NECTAR AND POLLEN MENU THROUGH THE YEAR

The best flowering plants for pollinators are ones with nectar- and pollen-packed anthers and stamens that haven't been turned into extra petals. Everything mentioned in this book—aside from a few double dahlias that I love and can't resist as cut flowers—is bee- and butterfly-friendly. It is well worth splitting up flowers through the year with pollinators in mind.

LATE WINTER TO EARLY SPRING

* **Bulbs** – Crocus, *Iris reticulata*, hyacinths, *Narcissus pseudonarcissus* 'Lobularis,' snake's head fritillary and muscari, single-flowering varieties of snowdrops, *Cyclamen coum*.
* **Shrubs and herbs** – Rosemary 'Miss Jessopp's Upright,' 'Tuscan Blue,' *Salix chaenomeloides* 'Mount Aso,' *Prunus incisa* 'Kojo-no-mai.'
* **Annuals** – *Cerinthe major*.
* **Perennials** – Hellebores 'Merlin,' 'Maestro,' and 'Green Corsican.'
* **Dandelions** – Especially loved by bumblebee queens!

LATE SPRING TO EARLY SUMMER

* **Bulbs** – Species tulips and scented ones, such as 'Ballerina' and 'Brown Sugar.'
* **Alliums** – All, but especially *Allium siculum* (syn. *Nectaroscordum siculum*) aptly known as Sicilian honey garlic, 'Purple Rain,' 'Purple Sensation,' *Cristophii*, and 'Violet Beauty,' Dutch iris, oriental lilies.
* **Perennials** – *Geum* 'Totally Tangerine' and 'Mai Tai,' oriental poppies, single roses such as 'Morning Mist,' perennial and annual wallflowers.
* **Annuals** – Borage, cornflowers, foxgloves, opium, and cornfield poppies.
* **Shrubs/trees** – Hawthorn, *Cotoneaster splendens*, holly and crab apple blossom along with other ornamental fruit bushes and trees, bramble blossom.

Crocus are especially spring sun-sensitive.

Salvias flower profusely through the summer and autumn.

MIDSUMMER TO EARLY AUTUMN

* **Dahlias** – 'Bishop's Children' and all Bishops, 'Totally Tangerine,' and 'Blue Bayou' are especially popular with butterflies.
* **Annuals** – Cosmos, tagetes, scabious, sunflowers, and Cape daisy.
* **Perennials** – Echinops, artichokes and cardoons, *Echium vulgare*, passionflowers, all buddleias, hollyhocks, marjoram, chives, sage, and lavender—the best for bees is considered to be a Downderry Nursery variety called 'Gros Bleu,' which in trials was found to be a favorite along with the traditional 'Hidcote.'
* **Evening perfume for moths** – Summer-flowering *Jasminum officinale* and *Jasminum × stephanense*, very classy evergreens for dressing walls and pillars with, single flowering roses, honeysuckles—*Lonicera* 'Graham Thomas' and *L.* 'Serotina' are especially suitable to be planted up through hedges or to quickly grow up generous trellis or fence panels. Smaller ones for pots that are bushy in habit are 'Chic et Choc' and 'Rhubarb and Custard.'

MID-AUTUMN TO EARLY WINTER

* **Annuals** – *Cobaea scandens*, sunflowers, rudbeckias, cosmos.
* **Perennials** – New England asters 'September Ruby' and 'Violetta,' Japanese anemones, ivy flowers.
* **Salvias and dahlias** – From starting to flower at their full force from summer, dahlias will continue until the first frosts or until the autumn days become damp and dark. Some salvias such as 'Ember's Wish' will battle on until true winter temperatures take hold if they are somewhere sheltered.

The New England class of asters flowers in autumn.

Echinops thistles remain some of the best flowers for bees.

A FLOWER YARD FOR BIRDS

Sometimes a garden's assets can be due to the gardens that neighbor it. I have long loved a holly tree that inhabits the corner of a neighbor's plot, and thanks to its songbird-attracting qualities, I think holly is the most magnificent of small trees; it teems with flitting visitors who tremble its leaves as they arrive and leave, and adorn it as if they were living Christmas decorations.

I love seeing birds in my garden and providing for them, as it creates an operatic wild aviary and the birds in turn provide some natural pest control among my plants. Blue tits are the most delicate and whimsical, with their unique lime-marmalade-yellow tummies; you can actively see them pecking over the emerging buds of roses in the spring, gathering up greenfly; their chicks especially need caterpillars that emerge with the opening of oak tree leaves. The robin, adorable but fierce, appears often to be alone, unless a pair has formed, and then it's almost impossible to tell the male from the female. She is a little larger and may be seen in the spring begging to be fed by the male as if she herself were a fledging. Quietly hopping about in the undergrowth, as they are ground feeders like the robin, are the flitting dunnocks, who seem to have the most docile characters of all. Again like the robin, they perform a chorus of the heavens but their tunes to our ears are often mistaken for those of the more decorative robins. We are lucky to get sparrows that live in a strict order of who feeds first: their arguments are almost constant, as is their spirited chirping that has disappeared from many gardens now.

The blackbirds appear to vanish for much of the summer and then return in the autumn in semi-tolerant flocks, the males strutting quickly on the ground with all the superiority that male peacocks adopt, acting like a gang of brothers one moment then chasing and sparring with each other with real venom the next. The brown females also suddenly turn on one another as their minds begin to think about nesting territories that are often hard won. What will draw them in well is the provision of an apple cut in half. On cold days I give them a stamped-on suet cake, placed either on the path or on one of the largest of the garden's pots, as they prefer to feed on the ground. The same goes for the robin, but he does eventually get the hang of feeding from a suspended suet cake by sitting on it and pecking.

A great deal of attention is rightfully being given to the importance of planting trees in gardens. For many birds, though, a thick garden hedge can

OPPOSITE Being inventive and sensible when it comes to feeding birds will be essential in not encouraging visits from squirrels who will delight in finding a typical bird feeder filled to the brim, especially in urban gardens. Here a metal tealight holder has been used to accommodate a suet cake. Viola 'Tiger Eye Red' can be seen in the background.

provide just as good, if not better, sanctuary. A favorite part of my hometown is a little narrow pathway that on either side has low hawthorn hedges—it's a songbird superhighway of activity. Recently, the bungalow on the other side of one of the hedges has been for sale. I wish that I could have afforded to buy it for the sake of ensuring that the old hedge remained. All such hedges I wish could be given serious preservation orders that are solidly noted on a house when it's listed for sale.

If you really think about it, though, it's not too hard to see why little garden birds like thorny-leaved shrubs and hedges—they provide a large amount of cover, so that the birds have natural protection from predators, safe nesting opportunities, and an abundance of food in the form of berries and aphids. All gardeners need to do, therefore, to be truly successful in attracting such delicate little winged jewels into their gardens is plant more such hedges.

Hawthorn is the best of all to create a hedge as it grows a dense thicket-like mesh that only birds can ping in and out of. Like roses, hawthorn hedging can be bought cheaply in the winter as bare-root plants. A mixed hedge of hawthorn, holly, ivy, honeysuckle, and the richly berried cotoneaster and pyracantha could all be planted into a cattle trough, where the young saplings, if their leading growth tips are trimmed off in the spring, will soon bush up. Alternatively, if any space in the ground is available then such a boundary would grow well and fast. It's worth remembering, too, that thorny hedges make very good defenses against people! If planting a hedge isn't possible, then fence panels can be made more attractive to birds by planting the clinging, climbing *Hydrangea petiolaris*, which will be happy in a large pot and quickly soften fenced boundaries without needing to be tied onto trellis or wires. Once this is established a honeysuckle or passionflower planted in a neighboring pot could be encouraged to snake and tangle through it. When spring arrives, be careful when removing hazel, bamboo canes, and birch that you may have staked tightly into a garden's corner, as often these temporary thickets have attracted a nest and if it is disturbed then its fate of being deserted is usually set.

Bird feeders can provide valuable dining for garden birds, especially over the winter months and during the spring and summer when adult birds need energy while they are rearing chicks and molting their feathers. To survive, a small bird such as a robin needs to eat between one-quarter and one-third of its body weight each day. On cold winter days, when the ground is frozen, both bird feeders and birdbaths are truly lifesaving.

OPPOSITE Perhaps unsurprisingly, winter provisions for songbirds will often help them get through winter's chill. Cold periods of frozen ground and snow will result in many birds visiting gardens to seek a meal that would otherwise be hard to find. Encouraging a good population of blue tits to visit the garden will have its reward as they love to eat aphids, which will begin to appear on buds as winter retreats. You'll see the birds delicately perch upon the thinnest and tiniest buds of roses inspecting each in turn for a meal of greenfly.

It is essential to clean a bird feeder often—in fact, it's highly irresponsible not to do so. Nature did not design tits and finches to poke through the metal and plastic hole entrances of bird feeders, so the ailments and pathogens that naturally affect songbirds increasingly plague uncleaned bird feeders. Diseases such as avian pox—a viral skin infection that causes alarming growths like blisters to appear through feathers—is now rapidly spreading through garden bird populations thanks to dirty bird feeders. There are riskier things they can catch, too, when dining out, such as Aspergillosis, avian influenza, and Trichomoniasis. With the tubular sort of bird feeder, the best way to clean it is to soak it in hot soapy water for a few hours, clean it with a little wire pipe brush, then let it dry.

The other issue of feeding birds in a small garden is, admittedly, the risk of attracting vermin. My great aunt Iris would say often, "Well, my neighbor feeds the birds and I get the rats!" And that's true if bird feeding is done without much thought. It should be about providing enough daily food that visiting birds eat everything and don't leave lots of bird feed hanging around uneaten. Full bird feeders left with lots of spilled seed will attract the unwanted, whether that's rats or squirrels, or wood pigeons, who are complete pigs really and their droppings in a small garden cause a right mess. To avoid this, I tend to feed loose suet cakes. I put one out daily, hanging it on the spike of a metal candleholder that is round and stands in a leafy corner of the garden under the neighbor's holly tree so that the birds don't feel exposed or are made to venture out into the open of the garden too much. On cold winter days, I often put out one in the morning and another around mid-afternoon, once the first has been eaten. Songbirds have busy times of feeding in the morning and late afternoon, when they must eat as much as they can as they digest their later meal overnight, which helps to keep them warm.

ABOVE Bees need water too, but they seem quite selective in their watering holes. If one is to their liking, however, entire hives of honeybees will visit it to take water back to their hive. A saucer filled with chicken grit so that the water is little more than 1cm (½ inch) deep may prove to be an acceptable bee bath.

OPPOSITE Shallow plant saucers of various sizes will be quickly used by birds to drink and bathe in so they should be scrubbed and refilled weekly. Those that are deeper will require some logs or large stones for access, and can be planted with sprigs of water mint. Even this meager offering in terms of water will be appreciated by frogs, who will then do an excellent job denting slug populations over the summer. The lily in flower here is 'Mister Cas.'

ORGANIC PEST CONTROL

Songbirds are the best organic control, but very few urban gardens attract populations as easily as rural ones do, so you will still need to assert organic control methods.

Slugs and snails – Beautifully smelling to us, slugs and snails dislike the natural saltiness of seaweed flakes. Use generously to cover emerging dahlias; shoots need to be sprinkled with a good 5cm (2 inches) of seaweed mounded around them. Another deterrent is smearing the rims of pots with a thick barrier of Vaseline®, though you will need to replenish it weekly. To strengthen defenses, salt can be applied on top of it, but beware that heavy rain will wash this off. You can gather them up using beer traps or orange and grapefruit halves at night. I find that coffee grounds give mixed and often unreliable results for slug protection despite the claims.

Aphids – If you discover a colony of blackfly or greenfly on a part of a plant, such as a dahlia stem, either wipe them off with a bit of tissue or dislodge them with a plant mister containing just water. Tagetes are good in a summer garden as their scent often repels aphids. Usually, though, aphids strike when plants are struggling and not in the best of health, so their presence could signal that something is wrong, such as under- or overwatering or feeding.

Vine weevils – These are the unseen plague of container gardens because the grubs silently eat the roots of plants within your pots and you will be unaware of the damage inflicted until the plant above suffers and dies. When buying plants at nurseries, always lift them out of their pots to inspect them for healthy and fibrous roots. Most gardens containing pots will have some vine weevils, but regular emptying out of the annual summer and bulb displays will dent populations. The adults emerge at night and can be caught and crushed, but nothing seems to eat them as they are built like army tanks. Their eggs and larvae can be dealt with by using a live culture of nematodes that you need to apply in late spring and early autumn.

Weeds – If you really can't bear the thought or look of plants self-seeding into paving cracks, then most annual weeds can be killed by spraying them on hot days with undiluted white vinegar, a cheap and wildlife-safe alternative to harmful chemical herbicides. Apple cider vinegar also works well.

PREVIOUS Allowing sunflowers and millets to go to seed will provide natural bird food.

ABOVE Aphids can be dislodged by hand or a handheld water spray. If you protect plants that slugs are especially fond of, and regularly inspect places they hide in, then a garden's population can be managed organically.

OPPOSITE Blackbirds are one of the most abundant British songbirds. However, starvation of chicks is a risk during dry weather as earthworms become impossible to find, so offer water-soaked mealworms during dry spells.

The more plants a pond of any size can have within it, be it a container one or traditionally dug, the better to assist in water chemistry and health.

I have all of these plants in a dolly tub that is quite deep, so the water lily sits on several upturned plastic plant pots, so it is about 40cm (16 inches) under the water's surface. The marginal plants that like to just paddle have their roots tied up in burlap bags and are then tied with fine string to the dolly tub's rim that helpfully has holes in it so the string can be threaded through, and the marginals then dangle in floating clumps. Oxygenating plants float within the water at will. My favorite—the luscious green *Elodea crispa* sold for goldfish adornment—is sadly now classed as illegal for fear it could be invasive, so the native hornwort is the one to opt for. A solar-powdered air pump will aid a container pond hugely over the summer and is vital if any goldfish are present. Unlike a fountain, the bubbling air stone will not upset a water lily, which will not thrive if its pads are splashed by a fountain: they like still waters. Both water movement and the presence of goldfish helpfully stop mosquito larvae that will quickly otherwise infest little pools over the summer months. The goldfish though need to be given to someone with a larger and deeper ornamental pond in the autumn due to the winter cold risk of them freezing in a container.

* **Water lily 'James Brydon'** – Lily pads help cover the water's surface, which helps to deter algae by blocking out excess sunlight. Bumblebees love the flowers that last two days and the lily pads let bees land on them to drink. Water lilies get better with age, flowering more the older they get. Remove the pads and deadhead the flowers as they fade, turning brown and yellow. The spent flowers can be told apart from the new buds by giving them a squeeze; they'll squirt water unlike the firm ones yet to open. Water lily pots should be well dressed with a topping of washed grit as they are submerged so that the aquatic compost doesn't puff out and murky the water.

* **Marginals** such as Iris Louisiana 'Black Gamecock,' water spearmint (*Mentha cervina*), water wint (*Mentha aquatica*)—the roots of marginals that paddle into the water act as a natural filter system helping to keep the water clean. Water mint is useful for even deep birdbaths or fountains, as it will grow in very shallow or simply damp places; just a sprig will quickly take root. Water forget-me-not has flowers reminiscent of the biennial land version.

* **Oxygenators** such as hornwort. Throw in and it will submerge just under the surface.

OPPOSITE Like wildflower meadows, wetlands have suffered a destruction of some 90 percent in the past hundred years in Britain, and those that remain are at high risk of pollution. Frogs especially are hugely helpful in gardens to patrol slug numbers. While a dolly tub would be too tall for them to access, lower metal containers such as tin baths or sinks that are watertight can be made accessible to them by piling up logs and stones around their edges. Ensure that all ponds have easy access for wildlife around their edges by planting marginal plants for them to rest on and crawl over. Placed branches are helpful for this too.

Spring

*Hope rewarded with the signs of proper life: full-on flower
regalia returns with clout and confidence as do the sight and sound
of bees and birdsong, rewarding the soul and heart when
it is often most needed. Dry springs will see pots needing to
be watered, especially small ones, but remember that such pots
can be brought into the house as living flower arrangements.
Be on guard still against squirrels as they'll eat tulip bulbs even
once they have sprouted and are growing well.*

Painted lady butterflies are migratory, flying at incredibly high altitudes from the fringes of northern
African deserts and the Middle East to eventually reach Europe by late spring. Until recently, much
of their almost 145,000km (9,000 mile) round trip was mysterious but studies done by the Butterfly
Conservation Trust have shown that the painted ladies that make it to gardens in the Northern
Hemisphere are not the same ones that began this long journey but are their descendants, in fact
it takes six successive generations to make the full trip. For such migrations to continue, a feast
of nectar-rich and pesticide-free flowers in gardens, providing something like butterfly motorway
service stations, are essential!

Opposite: Crocus 'Orange Monarch' and 'Flower Record' with the iris 'Purple Hill.'

Before the tulips—late winter and early spring

The key to success for growing tulips is to use pots with good drainage holes, provide protection from squirrels, and water often during the spring when the weather is dry.

As beautiful and glamorous as tulips are, I have learned not to allow them to eclipse all other spring bulb planting. It's well worth remembering that you need pots to begin awakening with good pools of color when your eyes and mind arguably need to be stimulated the most, which is late winter and early spring (February and March in the UK). This is several weeks before most tulips begin to even show signs of flower buds; their promising green beaks will have broken the soil's surface, but this is not enough zap for what can seem like endless gray days of late winter.

Each new winter and spring are quickly—like all seasons—becoming less and less predictable and making it harder for sleeping bumblebees and honeybees to know what the season is telling them. Sudden odd warm spells in January, February, and March (September, October, and November in the Southern Hemisphere) will mean pollinators will awaken earlier. Gardens therefore need to have a good number of flowers ready and waiting to greet them as late winter and spring cocktails, even though within hours winter can return and the flowers that in the same day were a haven of open faces and excitable buzzing guests may be surrounded by gathering snowflakes. The old saying of "Ne'er cast a clout till May be out," reminding us of the fickleness of British weather, has never been more apt in a world where climate change is rapidly picking up its pace.

Smaller, diamond-like bulbs, such as irises and crocuses, when planted generously in pots, are incredibly effective en masse, especially if you focus and group the pots that you plant them in together in a place where you can see them each day from indoors. This is why putting effort into having delicate and intimate mixed-bulb lasagnas (see page 90) within pots placed as stages on a garden table is worth the thought, because in such a location they really have a huge impact when the rest of the garden is still waking up and just dark, black soil. If you are on a bulb budget then it is better to focus on planting bulbs in pots that are visible from the house and let the other pots in the garden slumber.

ABOVE The Dutch iris 'Red Ember' and 'Eye of the Tiger' flower in early summer, and are planted in the autumn. They are cheap and very perennial bulbs but their foliage emerges early and becomes quite messy by the time flowering occurs so I only combine these bulbs with crocus and narcissi to allow breathing room for all concerned.

OPPOSITE The spring iris 'Purple Hill' with in-bud hyacinths 'Woodstock' and muscari.

The benefit of restricting yourself to just earlier-flowering bulbs and leaving tulips from their bulb lasagna combination is, firstly, that the smaller bulbs—and any plants growing above them, especially violas—won't get smothered by the emerging tulips as they grow upward. And secondly, all spring bulbs apart from tulips really want to be planted so that they can begin growing their roots before the end of October (mid-autumn). Snake's head fritillary bulbs and *Narcissi poeticus* (commonly called pheasant's eye) especially are better if they can be planted in the early autumn.

I don't endlessly do bulb lasagnas in all my pots anymore, but bulbs that are earlier and shorter in height than tulips are ensured a place in a few pots that take center stage—circular, quite low, old tin baths or low terracotta bowls, aptly often titled bulb bowls, suit these combinations well as there is good plant-to-pot height symmetry. As always, odd numbers work best for grouping pots on a table—three or five in a line, possibly even seven, in a zigzag of large to smaller, end to end. Alternatively, just one especially large round pot will do a good job when placed alone in the middle of a table.

The thing to do once these earlier bulbs go over, if they are not to be planted with tulips, is to plant violas or kale on top of them, as the violas will be in full flower once the early flowering bulbs fade away. If not, then ideally shove these bulb bowls into a hidden corner of the garden where they can brown off, happily storing up the energy they need for next year's flowers. The reality of a small garden, though, is that there often isn't space for

PREVIOUS Bringing the most scented bulbs inside in their pots rather than cutting them for the vase will see them last far longer as living arrangements. So plant some of your bulbs in small pots that can be brought into the house, provided that they are kept well watered. If they can be put outside for a few hours so much the better as spring flowers won't last in hot rooms. *Narcissi poeticus* (left) and hyacinth 'Woodstock' (right).

BELOW The cheerful faces of violas—'Envy' (left), 'Sorbet Honey Bee' (center), 'Irish Molly' (right).

suddenly fading pots to be moved to, so kales save the day and prevent what was a huge carnival from suddenly looking completely dead. The kales in question need to be grown from seed. I sow them in late summer, so they are nice little plants that get planted on top of the freshly planted bulb lasagnas.

By the end of late spring (May in the UK), you can rediscover these pots and—for bulbs that will reliably return, so can be left in—brush off the dried chaff left by the foliage. This applies to almost every bulb apart from tulips, but even with these there are exceptions (see the list of best perennial varieties on page 85). If you don't want the faff of emptying out the pots of the bulbs at all then you can direct sow a scattering of seeds through them, such as *Linaria* or perhaps *Nigella*, California poppy, calendula, or *Cerinthe major*, so that the pots can again take to a stage in the garden by late summer. Such seeds won't mind the spent compost provided they are watered well as they establish and the seed is scattered onto a roughed-up soil surface.

ABOVE If the growth tips are pinched out as seedlings, then violas will bush out well. A single plant of viola 'Sorbet Tiger Eye' (left), content in a small terracotta pot, perfect to be taken into the house as a living arrangement for the weekend, and pansy 'Frizzle Sizzle Burgundy' (right).

BULBS FOR LATE WINTER AND EARLY SPRING CHEER

These are essential little diamonds of hope; the more the merrier and they'll reappear each spring for evermore too.

Crocus – 'Orange Monarch' is expensive, but this is spring's version of true gold. Each tiny flower will sing out on dull days like canary beaks and then, in the first rays of spring sunshine, glow like little flames. This is one of my favorite bulbs, but as it's tiny you can't be too generous with the number planted. For bigger flowers, go for the cheaper 'Flower Record.' On sunny days the flowers open to display the best orange stamens.

Iris reticulata – I often feel sorry for these delicate, fledgling-like hummingbird chicks that find themselves emerging into winter's last hurrah, because if the season is harsh and windy, these little ones struggle. When I go a year without them, I miss them. They look and return very well if planted into grass each year and will also return if planted into permanent pot displays or lifted and kept in a plastic pot somewhere in a forgotten corner and aren't allowed to dry out and shrivel up. I love their delicate little flags of upright petals looking like the crests of exotic cock pheasants, and despite me making them sound like they are too tender to bother with, they are in fact made of hardier stuff and will dust themselves off when the spring sun breaks through the sky. Of varieties, I return to either 'Harmony,' which is of royal blue, or 'Purple Hill,' which is of the best hummingbird iridescent purple.

Hyacinths – It's worth having trios of hyacinths in pots that are of a modest size as well as having them in large pots of mixed lasagnas. These can be brought into the house to be dressed with a moss top layer (see page 79) and the stems propped up with a few little twigs that will stop the blooms from quickly taking on the appearance of drunks from the warmth of central heating. Their perfume is so beautiful that it must be enjoyed both indoors and indeed by the door. I love everything about them; they are daft creatures most of them, in their first year they are so big and heavy that they flop, or the wind snaps them, but they make a good cut flower. Unfortunately, some people don't like the scent, in which case you won't wish to have them! Of all varieties, 'Woodstock' is my favorite, as it is of an incredible cut-beetroot color, being a deep scarlet rather than purple. I have been tempted by the marvelously named 'Gipsy Queen,' but don't be fooled by photos as it is not a banana-milkshake yellow or even a dusty orange but a rather dull peach. 'Jan Bos' is of *EastEnders*' Pat Butcher neon-pink lipstick, of far better garish clout.

PREVIOUS 'Tiger Eye' violas and 'Frizzle Sizzle Burgundy' pansies massed into an old syrup tin (left) and Viola 'Tiger Eye Red' (right).

OPPOSITE Orange and warm-yellow crocus are especially welcome colors in late winter. This one is *Chrysanthus* var. *fuscotinctus*.

Narcissus poeticus (**pheasant's eye**) – A late to flower elegant narcissi, carrying a delicate cinnamon perfume from their orange and red centers and the most beautiful chiffon-like petals that are white yet carry just a touch of yellow vanilla pod to them. I wouldn't want tons of white in the garden, but for the scent having one pot filled with them is worth it. They make beautiful and very good cut flowers, but a pot planted with them alone can be brought into the house and look stunning. Plant as soon as you can in the autumn to ensure excellent flowering. Another narcissus in terms of equal elegance is 'Lobularis.' Known as the Lent lily daffodil, its soft-lemon petals will banish any snobbery associated with its rubber-duck-yellow kin.

Snake's head fritillary – These are amazingly inexpensive little popcorn-like bulbs, which is surprising given how exotic their flowers look. You'd think they would be much more expensive, but fortunately they are cheaply cultivated. Their flowers, which emerge from the center of smooth, thin, leek-like leaves, are unique, hanging-lantern-like creations that look as if they are from the fairy world of Queen Mab or Tolkien's Middle-earth. They have largely disappeared from the wild in the UK because plowing ruins the bulbs, shattering them to pieces within seconds. Dandelions outcompete them easily too, so finding them in wildflower meadows now is rare. They do, though, have some precious strongholds left. It is believed that 80 percent of their population left in Britain is within a floodplain covering some precious 44 hectares (108 acres) known as the North Meadow in Cricklade, North Wiltshire, sited along the River Thames. Each winter, the river vitally floods the fields and each summer they are harvested for their hay in an ancient management scheme known as Lammas, which thankfully is to the fritillaries' liking. In mid-spring (early April in the UK), the meadows begin to sparkle with their nodding flowers, by the middle of the month, in a year that is kind with some traditional April rain and not too much intense premature summer heat, the fritillaries bloom en masse, scattered like a marzipan of twinkling diamonds for around two weeks, during which time they are pollinated, especially by red-tailed bumblebees.

They like heavy, wet soil and maintain their magic far more when planted into a lawn, but even though they aren't really designed to be in containers I can't resist planting at least some in pots, overplanting them with Viola 'Tiger Eye Red,' whose flowers open under them excitably.

Muscari – I adore these more each year because the bees love them so much. They multiply happily, making them nice and cheap to buy and you do want quite a few to ensure impact. The best of them is *Muscari latifolium*; it's the most sophisticated combination of juicy grape blue fading to midnight navy. All the others of the class don't do it for me despite a lot of newly bred ones, as they are all of baby pink or nursery pastel blue.

Alliums – These wonderful flowers are the disco balls of the garden—full of nectar for bees. Their faded flowers make wonderful seedhead decorations for Christmas, so they are very giving. They don't, however, suit bulb lasagna mixes especially well, as their floppy leaves drown out other bulbs. It's best, therefore, to plant trios of allium bulbs in bucket-sized pots and enjoy them as exclusive displays. You can take off the strappy leaves as soon as they begin to look tired (they'll dangle over the pot looking very drunk), as the removal of them will not harm the bulbs. A good combination of height and sizes is to mix *Allium schubertii* 'Magic' and *A. cristophii* together; the latter often keeps a hint of its purple tint even when it's dried.

'Purple Sensation' is popular and the earliest allium, blooming in late spring, often meeting the late tulips in neighboring pots and complementing them, but I don't save this one for drying because it makes such a mess chucking its seeds all over, even when only gently touched! A favorite of bumblebees is the allium bulb aptly known as Sicilian honey garlic, *Allium siculum*. If planted generously—about seven bulbs—in a single pot they will spur up together, becoming quite tall and airy, then from their pointed buds their bell-like flowers will open and hang down like chandeliers and the bees will then dance frantically under them, drunk on their nectar.

LEFT The firework, sea urchin, sparkler *Allium schubertii*. This is the best bulb to plant with Christmas in mind as it looks like an incredible star once it has dried to a seedhead. In a pot, the leaves will look messy so these can be trimmed off without damaging the bulb as soon as their green starts to fade to yellow.

OVERLEAF *Muscari latifolium*, a favorite with bees and wonderfully cheap for filling both large and small pots alike. It has finer leaves than other muscari and if it's allowed to go to seed, the dried seedpods will scatter themselves into the cracks of paving and bricks. On the right is a favorite Barbu d'Uccle bantam hen, an especially small breed of true bantam whose foot feathers are helpful to limit scratching.

When to plant a bulb lasagna

What is good about tulips—provided the bulbs are stored somewhere dry and cold, such as in a mouseproof porch or shed—is that they can be planted as the New Year begins (so early January in the UK) and they will still flower perfectly well. So, in the UK at least, they can be given as Christmas presents to be swiftly planted early in the New Year. In a usual year (though that is becoming increasingly difficult to predict) tulip bulbs do not seriously begin to grow roots until the middle of January. Giving themselves so little time between awakening and flowering to store any energy in their original mother bulb is, however, one reason why they aren't often perennial.

If, however, you want to mix your tulips with other bulbs in a lasagna, you won't be able to delay so long, because the other bulbs—narcissi, iris, crocus, muscari, fritillaries, and hyacinth—require an earlier planting for assurance of a successful display. All these bulbs, unlike tulips, prefer to stir into life beneath the soil's surface as early as September (early autumn), and it's why they are far more perennial in habit than tulips are.

Worry, though, will reign here for the beginner gardener, who will have been correctly told that it is best to plant tulip bulbs after the first hard frost of the winter, because it helps deter viruses, such as tulip fire. What, therefore, is one to do for a bulb lasagna where all the bulbs need to be planted at the same time? A compromise must be made and, as tulips are always the deepest layer, I throw out this fear of planting tulips too early and plant mixes of bulbs earlier for the sake of the other early-to-awaken bulbs. So ideally plant mixed bulb lasagnas during late autumn (early November in the UK) and tulip-only pots during the darkest, short days of January; it's a nice task to do in the gloom of mid-winter. It can be easier to leave tulips out of a bulb mix altogether when it comes to delicate bulbs such as snake's head fritillaries, which may be smothered if there are too many broad tulip leaves.

OPPOSITE The early tulip 'Palmyra'—growing with the wallflower 'Sugar Rush Orange' and also kale 'Redbor'—almost coming into flower. The fact it was sown the previous summer stops it from becoming a large plant. The late tulip 'Black Parrot' will be in flower as 'Palmyra' drops her petals.

OVERLEAF An old version of the flower yard with a lot of tulips—today I would plant fewer tulips and a more diverse selection of bulbs for more tapestry and nectar diversity.

🌱 A PERENNIALLY RETURNING BULB LASAGNA WITH NO TULIPS

This is best planted from early autumn (mid-September in the UK) and is ideal for overplanting with violas.

* Crocus 'Orange Monarch' and 'Spring Beauty'
* Iris 'Purple Hill'
* Snake's head fritillary
* Hyacinth 'Woodstock'
* *Muscari latifolium*
* *Narcissus poeticus* (pheasant's eye)

The time of the tulip

No flower commands such addiction or stands with such effortless single perfection either singularly, like a displaying male bird-of-paradise, or en masse, like a flock of parading flamingos. Ideally you should plant enough to create visual impact in your pots and for picking.

MY FAVORITE TULIP BULB LASAGNA RECIPES

These tulips can also all be combined with the bulbs mentioned on pages 85–87.

Combine five, seven, or fifteen of each variety listed, depending on the size of your pot, and mix the singularly-bagged varieties together in a bucket before planting to ensure a natural look. All of them will be complemented by overplanting, especially with a mixed layer of *Iris reticulata* and crocus.

An extravagant mix of early, mid-season, and late-flowering tulips of stained-glass colors

I plant these every season as they are my trusted favorites in the garden and the vase alike.

✳ 'Palmyra' ✳ 'Black Parrot' ✳ 'Rococo' ✳ 'Irene Parrot' and/or 'Parrot King' ✳ 'Ballerina' ✳ 'Brown Sugar'

A reliably early to mid-season and late tulip mix of good height and plum-pudding, country-house, velvet-curtain colors

✳ 'Palmyra' – *tall, mid-season* ✳ 'Rococo' – *short, early* ✳ 'Artist' – *short, mid-season* ✳ 'Black Parrot' – *tall, late*

A lily-flowered trio—especially elegant with their curving and fluted petals

✳ 'Ballerina' – *very good when overplanted with geum* ✳ 'Totally Tangerine' ✳ 'Sarah Raven' and/or 'Burgundy' ✳ 'Request'

A classic orange and plum mix

These are all single tulips so are good for bees.

✳ 'Ronaldo' ✳ 'Prinses Irene' ✳ 'Brown Sugar' ✳ 'Black Parrot'

Best tulips for a scent like that of freesias

Both of these orange tulips are open, single varieties, so they are good for welcoming bees. They work well mixed with narcissi that have burnt-orange to almost-red corona trumpets. Such mixes would also give a good length of successional flowering and a divine scent.

✳ 'Ballerina' ✳ 'Brown Sugar'

Best narcissi to mix with orange tulips for scent

✳ 'Cragford' ✳ *N. poeticus* var. *recurvus* ('Old Pheasant's Eye') ✳ 'Geranium' ✳ 'Actaea' ✳ 'Lobularis,' or the lent lily daffodil

OPPOSITE Choose tulips to combine for different heights and early to late flowers. 'Irene Parrot' (above left) is late and quite short so helpful to give the pot some heart, 'Palmyra' (above right) is early and tall, 'Black Parrot' (below left) late and interesting even in bud, and 'Brown Sugar' (below right) is early, large, and beautifully scented.

An especially crazy and somewhat garish mix of tulips for fabulous cutting

These all look good as single picked stems or massed together in a vase with an open, fluted, collared rim that allows them to go all swan-necked; twirling and flopping as they wish, reminiscent of Dutch still-life paintings. If I ever have an allotment I will plant them in rows and embrace their clownish, crazy bravado, a total wonderful rabble. Otherwise, plant them in small terracotta pots as either singles, pairs, or trios of bulbs for the purpose of bringing them into the house as living flowers, but remember that such small pots will need frequent watering for them to flower successfully. They will need to be of a decent weight, too, to prevent the tulips toppling over, as these are tall varieties.

❉ 'Flaming Parrot' and/or 'Texas Flame'
❉ 'Helmar' ❉ 'Rem's Favourite' ❉ 'Estella Rijnveld' ❉ 'Grand Perfection'

Tulips as peonies—for spring weddings

These tulips look just like peonies, due to their profuse petals, so are of great help to the cut-flower calendar before peonies come into season. However, their profuse petals also mean they are sterile, so are of no benefit to pollinators. They range from traditional pastel pink to deep claret and copper-pink colorations. Plant a dozen of each bulb and you'll have a homegrown bridal bouquet of exceptional value and long vase life, worthy

of *Vogue*, and all without any air miles.
❉ 'Copper Image' ❉ 'La Belle Époque'
❉ 'Palmyra' ❉ 'Chato' ❉ 'Angelique'

Best tulips to expect to flower again the following year

The first five varieties carry flashes of green in
their petals, so as a group they are known as
Viridiflora. This class is known for being the most
reliable of tulip repeat-flowerers, doing so for
several years after being planted, especially if
planted in the ground, though they will also do
well in pots if planted deeply and allowed to die
back after flowering. For those on a budget, or
who don't want to plant tulips as an annual affair,
this is the group to invest in. The latter two
varieties are triumph tulips.

❉ 'Artist' ❉ 'Orange Marmalade' ❉ 'Purple Dance'
❉ 'Green Dance' ❉ 'Green Wave' ❉ 'Abu Hassan'
❉ 'Slawa'

PREVIOUS The classic
tulip 'Ballerina,' known for
its elegance and perfume.
Here the bulbs have been
planted under the hardy
perennial geum 'Totally
Tangerine.'

OPPOSITE A collection of
small terracotta pots with
snake's head fritillary and
the orange species tulip
orphanidea. Such small
pots need to be watered
every few days from late
winter into spring to
ensure they flower well.

RIGHT Tulip 'Artist'
(above)—unique in its
ripening nectarine
coloration—and 'Golden
Artist' (below) are both
especially perennial tulips.

OVERLEAF Planting some
of your large pots with just
early crocus bulbs, and no
tulips, allows for winter-
sown sweet peas to be
planted out in peak tulip
time. Here (left) smooth,
flexible stems of sapling
and self-seeded silver birch
have been used as sweet
pea wigwams. The tulips
are 'La Belle Époque,'
'Dream Touch,' and 'Black
Hero.'

Saving bulbs from squirrels

The bold tree rat that is the gray squirrel is a plague of many bulbs in pots, especially tulips and crocus. Once they know that bulbs are available they will eat all of them and cause much mess while doing so. Squirrels will be immediately curious of any pots that have been freshly planted and in the autumn they will be looking for places to use as stores for acorns and walnuts they have foraged. Any bare and freshly planted pots will therefore hold an instant attraction for them.

You can help make your freshly planted bulb lasagna pots less inviting by foraging the prickly stems of holly, blackthorn, or hawthorn and then pushing these stems into the top of the pot so that the surface resembles a thick, sharply thorned bush. You can also use the clippings of roses and brambles but this protection will only be successful if the prickly stems are placed closely together and pushed so deeply into the pot that determined squirrels cannot simply claw the stems off the pot's surface.

Other protective measures to consider include the metal dome bases of upturned hanging baskets. Firmly secured into the pot using tent pegs, they can then act like cloches, which is useful for pots that have been overplanted with growing plants, such as violas, as they can grow through the dome of mesh. Florist chicken wire that is painted black or dark green can be ordered and pegged down in the same fashion. It looks less visible than the unpainted, shiny galvanized wire but sometimes squirrels can bite through this if they are especially determined. Chile flakes also work well when they are applied thickly, like icing sugar, and continually reapplied every few weeks throughout the winter. To me, though, they look as if someone has been sick over the pot's surface, so for containers that are closely visible by the door, I don't like to use this method!

Squirrels will sometimes still eat tulips once they have sprouted, so knowing when to remove the protection needs to be finely judged. Usually, once the cold of winter has properly passed, there will be more for squirrels to eat, so unless you are especially plagued by these pests, tulips should be safe from early spring (the middle of March in the UK) onward.

ABOVE AND OPPOSITE
Sprigs of needle-sharp holly must be pushed into the surface of freshly planted pots of bulbs quite thickly for it to be effective against the paws and investigations of squirrels. Here the holly protects iris 'Harmony' (above) and hyacinth 'Woodstock' (opposite).

✿ BULBS RESISTANT TO SQUIRRELS

These all taste nasty due to their natural toxins, so although squirrels might disturb the pots when you have freshly planted the bulbs, crucially they won't eat the bulbs.

* Narcissi * Muscari * Alliums
* Hyacinths

Summer

Summer can be oddly stressful, because of the constant watering and feeding, and going away from your pots can leave them vulnerable so enlisting help will be essential to ease concern. Nights are long and those that are warm should be spent outside. Scent is at large in the heat, especially in the evenings, and the garden at such a time is at its most romantic. If things are too much in terms of effort, reduce the pot numbers and cut yourself some slack.

Hot summer days and the presence of salvias and *Verbena bonariensis* will see the most magical of pollinators—the hummingbird hawk-moth—appear like a fairy darting from flower to flower. These daytime flying moths flap their wings at around eighty-five times per second as they drink nectar. The swallowtail butterfly is not alas usually seen in many British gardens as it is largely to be found in the fenlands of the Norfolk Broads. Its caterpillars require the wild milk parsley plants that grow here.

Opposite: Salvia 'Ember's Wish' with *Verbena bonariensis* growing in large containers with *Panicum capillare* 'Sparkling Fountain.'

Salvias and roses—a traditional and modern companionship

The garden at Perch Hill, in East Sussex, created by Sarah Raven, is unique because its flower beds are often deliberate planting experiments, but it is all done so elegantly and with such gusto that visitors seldom realize this. One of the most successful experimental pairings of plants done there is the underplanting of roses with what were, until a few years ago, a fairly new group of salvias. These have a busy habit, with fine stems of small leaves and tiny but profuse flowers, each shaped like two plush-velvet love hearts put back-to-back and fluttering outward from their pointed ends, creating simple little flowers of upward hoods and downward bibs. This group of salvias is known as the *greggii* and *microphylla* hybrids, or as the small or baby leaf salvias.

Traditionally, companion planting has been focused on the vegetable garden and greenhouse, with good reason. The scent of tagetes (French marigolds), for example, is well known for repelling white fly from tomatoes. Less attention has been paid to the benefits of companion planting for plants prized for their flowers rather than their edible bounty. A whole array of resultant organic gardening plant marriages probably awaits discovery, to the benefit of gardener and plant health alike.

The scent of *microphylla* salvias on a hot summer day is one of pepper or, to some noses, of blackcurrant cordial. This fragrance, rising in the air to the waiting stems of roses above, seems to provide the latter with a natural perfume that repels several fungal issues commonly found to affect roses, most notably black spot. Black spot is the age-old nemesis of the rose lover. Like most plant ailments, it is triggered by stress caused either by underwatering or underfeeding, or both. If a rose becomes affected over the summer, then every leaf becomes bruised with dark green circles that ripen to become black spots. You can delicately strip off the affected leaves then remove them to the green waste bin so they are taken away from your garden. This will result in your rose looking as if it's been stripped by a visiting giraffe's tongue for a good month before it rebuds, if time within the summer season allows. A far better solution is to enlist the help of salvia scent and grow them below roses over the entire year. In pots, salvias make good partners to roses, billowing and frothing out, adding interest and fizz.

OPPOSITE The small, sage-leaved *Salvia × jamensis* lends itself to being planted in pots, growing into billowing and generously flowering clouds, with or without roses for them to consort with. They require sunny places, they cope well with the wind and prove to be drought-tolerant once they have established. For them to survive a cold winter no pruning should happen until late spring. Here are *Salvia × jamensis* 'Velvet Gem' (above left), and 'Nachtvlinder' (above right), and picked stems of 'Velvet Gem' and 'Nachtvlinder' with varieties 'Amethyst Lips,' 'Peach Cobbler,' and 'Wine and Roses' (below left). The rose 'Hot Chocolate' with a surround of *Salvia × jamensis* 'Nachtvlinder' (below right).

ROSES IN POTS

Roses do best in pots that are at least 46cm (18 inches) deep by 46cm (18 inches) wide, though the bigger the better. A pot this size would accommodate one rose underplanted with two *microphylla* varieties of salvias. Use a generous mix of John Innes No. 3 compost mixed with molehill soil and well-rotted organic manure, plus a top-dressing of organic manure each spring. Do not cut the salvias hard back until mid-spring, when all risk of frost has passed.

For roses in pots to thrive, they need to be watered often, as much as once a day during the heat of summer. An evening mist from a water sprayer of Uncle Tom rose tonic (which is free from chemicals and high in potassium phosphite) on the leaves each week in spring as they emerge, will ensure especially healthy growth, as will comfrey tea and seaweed feed. When deadheading or picking roses for the vase, always go down to a pair of leaves to promote fresh growth and more flowering.

The best time of year to plant roses is during the winter, when rose growers lift their fields of dormant roses and the largest choice of varieties is available in bare-root form. Most are then supplied by mail order. Bare-root roses are much cheaper than potted ones and become established better too. When planting either a bare-root or potted rose, the grafting union—a large, fist-like callous between the rose's root system and stems—should be below the surface of the soil, to prevent the rose from producing suckers (triffid-like upright stems that don't add to the attractive form of the rose's main structure). When planted, therefore, a bare-root rose should resemble a buried hand, with just its fingers sticking out of the soil! You can gift bare-root roses as Christmas presents, if they are stored in a cold shed or porch, wrapped in a damp cloth or newspaper, and kept in a bucket until a good frost-free day in the New Year allows for them to be planted. Soak the roots in a bucket of water for a few hours prior to planting.

When selecting a rose from a catalog, the words to take note of are "repeat flowering," meaning that you'll get a least an early and a late summer flush of flowers, and "good disease resistance." Unfortunately, although beautiful, a number of older varieties are not as disease resistant as more newly bred roses, and many are coping so poorly with climate change that they are no longer going to be grown commercially. However, the sheer variety of recent rose breeding means that in terms of looks newly bred varieties can now be easily matched to resemble beloved old ones, so all is not lost.

🌱 BEST BEE-FRIENDLY ROSES

✳ *Rosa × odorata* 'Mutabilis' – This flowers longer than almost any other rose. The simple, silk-like flowers are every shade of deep to pale pink to an almost coral orange. It has beautiful foliage, too.

✳ 'Wild Rover' – A classic, wild-looking rose of rich purple-crimson. Very healthy and fast growing. Newly bred and of a deeper, almost-purple ruby is 'Night Owl.'

✳ 'Morning Mist' – A David Austin, repeat-flowering shrub rose with single flowers of rich coral and a good, upright, spurring habit.

🌱 BEST REPEAT-FLOWERING ROSES FOR CUTTING AND PERFUME

✳ 'Hot Chocolate' – Rich terracotta orange, upright and strong growth.

✳ 'Summer Song' – Coral; a very good drape-like habit for fences.

✳ 'Timeless Purple' – Velvet dark purple, strong upright growth.

✳ 'Calendar Girl' – A sultry pink tutu of a rose, the color of summer fruits and jelly-soaked trifle sponge!

ABOVE *Rosa × odorata* 'Mutabilis' (left), rose 'Morning Mist' (center), and rose 'Calendar Girl' (right). For roses to thrive in pots watering and feeding need to be generously supplied over the spring and summer months.

OVERLEAF An old dustbin with the summer froth of *Salvia × jamensis* 'Nachtvlinder,' the result of three 9cm (3½ inch) cuttings being planted that spring.

Sweet peas

Sweet peas offer perfume and prolific bursts of annual color, and they are superb cut flowers. They are also bee friendly. If they are being grown in a pot it needs to be as large and deep as possible, filled with a soil as rich as you can create. When preparing a pot that is either a dustbin or a large container, I mix a quarter compost and a quarter molehill soil, then the other half of the mix is a very well-rotted organic manure or (if you can't get such manure easily) for every two large garden spades' worth of compost going into the pot, add a generous handful of comfrey pellets or organic chicken manure. Please only buy organic chicken manure pellets so you are not buying a by-product of cruel, intensive battery farming.

Sweet peas require a 2m (7 foot) tall wigwam or wall trellis to climb up. You can make this out of bamboo canes, or it can be a metal structure, but both will be too slippery for the little peas to climb on their own, so provide them with several gathered little sticks around the base of the wigwam when they are planted out as their clinging tendrils will easily be able to wrap around these to help them get started. The tendrils will also like the feeling of twine, which you can tightly zigzag through the bamboo canes.

What sweet peas love to climb up the most though are the stems of silver birch. Despite the name, sapling silver birch will willingly self-sow on wasteland and isn't silver as a feral infant but a varnished brown. They are firmly upright and twiggy, perfect for creating wigwams with. These young saplings can be foraged, cutting them down to about halfway, provided that it is done over the winter when they are dormant and it therefore won't harm them. Hazel also works very well as a sweet pea wigwam and will be available as bundles to buy from coppiced managed woodland or even some garden centers. Coppicing supports a wide array of woodland wildflowers by creating a light-filled woodland canopy.

As annual climbers, sweet peas need a degree of sun but arguably not full. They do not cope well in especially hot weather, as it gets the better of them, encouraging their icing-sugar, fungal nemesis that is powdery mildew to strike. Climate change is making sweet peas a more fleeting presence for the garden's early summer show, and their season may need to move swiftly toward autumn in years to come if British summertimes continue to become hotter than they traditionally have been in the past. Sowing sweet peas in late spring (the middle of May in the UK) will ensure an autumn show of them.

ABOVE Before there are any flowers, pinching out sweet pea growth tips when they are little seedlings is essential to ensure bushy plants that produce plenty of flowers (top). Once there are flowers, picking tendrils that have not clung to supports helps the sweet peas devote energy to flowers (below).

OPPOSITE A sweet pea tapestry in Bristol blue vases, including varieties 'Matucana,' 'Windsor,' 'Black Knight,' 'Beaujolais,' 'Eclipse,' 'America,' and 'King Edward VII.'

SOWING SEED

There is a lot of debate as to what sweet pea seeds should be sown into. Sweet peas are legumes, and as all members of this plant group like to grow long roots, I sow my seeds in root trainers, which provide them with a nice long channel. I also find having them standing together tightly upright makes them easy to manage. Filling them is an art and consists of piling the compost on top of the tubes, mounding it until they all seem to be full, then lifting the root trainer setup entirely and then thudding it down so that the compost properly fills each cell. You do this several times, then you can take a hand brush and sweep off the excess compost. I say compost, but lately I've found that sweet peas especially thrive from the outset when sown into compost mixed at a ratio of 50:50 with molehill soil!

I do, though, know several very good growers of sweet peas who just sow seed in standard 9cm (3½ inch) square pots with good success. Traditionally toilet-roll tubes were used, and these still work well, but they do quickly begin to fall apart as they become damp through watering.

Whatever you sow your sweet peas in, it's best to start them off inside as indoor heat will speed up their germination. They will germinate in an unheated greenhouse or cold frame, but if it's chilly the seed will take much longer to germinate, and it may rot before it can do so.

The last flush of the sweet peas will be so short in length it's hardly worth picking them. Let these pods fade to brown if you can, and keep watering the plants so the seedpods swell and feel fat. At this point you can pick them and save them for your own sweet pea seed for sowing next year. Sweet pea seed that is more than three years old usually has a poor germination rate, though, so whatever you sow—whether bought or stored—make sure it is fresh.

ABOVE Sweet pea seed has a short shelf life. I do save some of my own seed at the end of each year, allowing the last pods to ripen and get fat, but I also buy seed of specific varieties. Good rates of germination do seem at times to be something of a seasonal lottery even from home-produced seed.

OPPOSITE Picking the seedpods only adds to the charms of a bunch of 'Matucana' and 'Lord Nelson.'

OVERLEAF The routine of filling and sowing sweet peas into root trainers. This, together with the protection of a cold frame, will produce healthy seedlings.

🌱 TOP TIPS FOR SEED SOWING

* Sow seeds singularly or in pairs, but don't ever disturb them by pricking them out from one another as they hate this and it will usually cause them to die. When it comes to transplanting seedling sweet peas, they need to be planted from their pots or root trainers into their final positions with minimum disturbance of their roots.

* Sow your sweet pea seeds between mid-autumn and late winter (October to February in the UK), as this will mean you have flowers for picking from the late spring to midsummer (May until July in the UK) depending on the heat over these months. To have sweet peas to pick in late summer and early autumn, sow some seed in late spring.

* Soak sweet pea seeds in an eggcup overnight. By the morning, the seeds should have swelled to at least double their original size; any that haven't plumped up or are floating I discard. The soaked seed needs to be sown within forty-eight hours to avoid rotting. Soaking speeds up germination but it isn't necessary; unsoaked seed just takes a little longer to germinate, whereas young growths usually begin to peek out from soaked seeds at about three weeks. If you have mice around, the seedlings will need to be protected; I use an old hamster cage to cover them!

* Push each seed down into the soil to the depth of your first knuckle of your finger. Almost as soon as the seedlings have raised their heads and are 2.5cm (1 inch) tall, place them outside under a cold frame or within a greenhouse—you need to provide slightly cooler temperatures to stall their top growth so that they focus on growing strong roots. Once the seedlings have four pairs of leaves, with your thumb and forefinger pinch out their growth tips so that they bush outward to form very stocky and strong plants.

* For a large container or dustbin-sized pot, plant five sweet pea plants—or one plant for each upright rod of the supporting wigwam. Feeding usually begins once the seedlings have climbed 30cm (12 inches) up the canes; sweet peas are very hungry plants and underfeeding will see them underperform, so do it weekly. Use comfrey or liquid seaweed: a generous glug or capful in the case of seaweed or a mug's worth of comfrey sloshed into a water-filled watering can.

* Pick the flowers as much as you can. This will stimulate more flowers to be produced. Cut sweet peas flop very quickly if they are out of water for long, so if taking bunches to friends do so in water-filled jam jars so they arrive well perked up rather than limp.

* When they become frazzled and their display is over, cut down the sweet peas from their supports but don't dig them out of the pot because their fibrous, deep-growing roots are very good for the soil's structure as they add nitrogen to it. A late-sown pumpkin is the perfect climber to replace the sweet pea in the pot to make use of the now-bare canes.

🌱 BEST VARIETIES BY SCENT

* 'Matucana' – One of the oldest sweet pea varieties, with unsurpassed perfume and small flowers of rich purple and indigo.

* 'Cupani' is almost identical to the wild sweet peas found in Sicily, so it is whimsically small but, like 'Matucana,' is strongly scented.

🌱 BEST VARIETIES BY COLOR

* 'Emilia Fox,' 'Purple Pimpernel,' 'Indigo King' – Are all like 'Matucana' in their colors but larger in their flower sizes, and they have taller stems. 'Lord Nelson' provides a more navy purple.

* 'Mark Williams,' 'Beaujolais,' 'Black Knight,' 'Windsor' – Rich burgundy and claret, satin, large-flowering varieties.

* 'King Edward VII,' 'Winston Churchill,' 'Henry Thomas' – Satin, flamenco, statement royal reds.

* 'Henry Eckford,' 'Prince of Orange,' 'Valerie Harrod' – The richest of corals to almost orange scarlets.

* 'Nimbus,' 'Wiltshire Ripple,' 'America' – Old-fashioned, marbled petals that jazz up any bunch and go surprisingly well with bolder colors when they are picked together.

PREVIOUS Annual sweet peas combined with the rich pink of perennial, everlasting sweet peas. Once established, if content, perennial sweet peas will drench fences beautifully with their flowers, although alas there is no scent from them.

ABOVE Sweet pea 'Matucana,' the most fragrant of all (left) and 'Black Knight,' a rich crimson-wine black variety (right).

OPPOSITE Sweet pea 'Emilia Fox,' one of the best of recently bred varieties as it has a large flower on a tall stem but still carries a good perfume.

Cosmos

No seed is more giving than cosmos. The dainty, floating but dramatic daisy-like flowers now come in such an array that there is one for every taste, but it is 'Rubenza,' of satin-red fading to bruised morello-cherry pink, that wins the prize for me. It doesn't become a greedy triffid like some of the other popular cutting cosmos, but it has a thin central stem and an airy dancing habit. Avoid the dwarf and compact varieties of cosmos, especially the Sonata Series, as these are dumpy plants in comparison to those bred with cut flowers in mind.

I sow cosmos in late spring and early summer because they grow very quickly. Fifteen little half-moon seeds should be spaced out into a seed tray so that each is several centimeters from its sibling, allowing the tray of seedlings to germinate and grow well into dangling, miniature, fern-like tree infants. When it comes to potting each one on into its own 9cm (3½ inch) pot the roots seem to sense immediately the expectations and romp away, forming a strong root ball. Three cosmos will go into a dustbin or large container coupled with a pair of the *Tagetes* 'Linnaeus Burning Embers' and millet 'Red Jewel' all sown in the same seed-tray fashion.

Any cosmos that by midsummer look as if they are growing thickly, like a piece of green Christmas tinsel, should be cut back to halfway because they need to be stimulated to produce flower buds rather than dense foliage. The constant cutting of cosmos down to a pair of leaves ensures they continually produce fresh flowers deep into the autumn.

There are some other varieties of cosmos that do well in pots too, especially the smaller, orange flowering ones such as 'Bright Lights Mixed,' which is reminiscent of buttercups! As seedlings these tend to take a little longer to get into their stride and they won't cope with being crowded by more rampant annuals in pots so plant them out into their final summer containers once they have grown to a good size within a 9cm (3½ inch) pot. The chocolate cosmos is more of a dahlia than a cosmos but it's an individual in any case, growing from a tuber rather than a seed. It can be potted up like a dahlia in late spring and makes for a beautiful single statement pot on a summer table. To overwinter a chocolate cosmos, cut back the foliage in late autumn and pot the tuber back into a 3 liter (5¼ pint) plastic pot as if you are planting it again in fresh compost. Then overwinter it somewhere dry and frost free, and it should begin to wake up and sprout by mid-spring.

OPPOSITE Cosmos 'Rubenza' being visited by honeybees (above left and below right) and growing with millet 'Red Jewel' (above right) and with cosmos 'Bright Lights Mixed' (below left). Cosmos are rarely troublesome provided they are pinched out as seedlings and their flowers are then picked to encourage more.

OVERLEAF *Tagetes* 'Linnaeus Burning Embers' taking center stage in bloom, as a French marigold bush (left). The dahlia in the foreground is the seed-grown dahlia 'Bishop's Children' (right).

Tagetes

The French marigolds, tagetes, have been major victims in the modern bedding-plant breeding programs where they have been turned typically into dumpy, heavy mop-headed little things forming the most grotesque brain-like, huge flowers for park-bedding schemes.

Thankfully, some varieties gate-crash this modern usual and grow far taller, up to 60cm (2 feet) tall in the case of 'Linnaeus Burning Embers' and 'Cinnabar.' By midsummer these are marigold bushes with flowers of yellow and orange middle stamens surrounded by velvet blood-orange and mahogany-colored petals. A little shorter but still just as profuse in a blossom of semi-double flower is 'Konstance,' which is superb as a cut flower and a little larger in bloom than its taller cousins.

Only a few seeds need to be sown as each will grow into a bushy plant, so just one seedling will romp away in a large pot accompanied by a cosmos 'Rubenza,' a scabious 'Black Cat,' and finally a consorting foliage trio of millet or panicum grass seedlings with them all flowering willingly with deadheading or better still being picked for the vase, always down to a pair of leaves to encourage fresh growth. Hoverflies—which are often neglected in celebrating pollinators, perhaps as they impersonate bees so superbly that untrained eyes are easily tricked—seem to adore tagetes flowers. The foliage of tagetes will perfume the garden wonderfully after a summer shower too and this scent will help to repel aphids.

ABOVE A bumblebee feeding from *Tagetes* 'Linnaeus Burning Embers.'

OPPOSITE As pollinators, hoverflies are often overlooked, easily mistaken for bees or wasps as their impersonations are often very good. But they have no sting, and also only have one pair of wings, unlike bees who have two pairs. There are around 280 species of hoverfly found in Britain and the larvae of some species do a helpful but largely unknown job of eating aphids. This one is known as the marmalade hoverfly, and is feeding from *Tagetes* 'Linnaeus Burning Embers.'

Scabious

Scabious are one of the most beautiful summer characters of a British wildflower meadow. The most often seen are the hardy perennial field scabious with their lilac pincushion blooms stacked full of pollen and nectar. It suits being introduced to both a garden lawn and perennial container very well. Echoing this wildflower but with more gusto and seemingly of an old-world elegance are the annual *Scabiosa atropurpurea*, the most divine being the mulberry jam-velvet 'Black Cat' or 'Black Knight' but they also come in a mix of confetti pastel colors as the aptly titled 'Tall Double Mix.' They will all grow to a height of between 90cm and 1.2m (3 and 4 foot) tall. Those with sheltered gardens may choose to sow scabious in the autumn, pricking out the seedlings and growing them under the protection of a cloche or greenhouse over the winter in 9cm (3½ inch) pots and then planting them into their final pot positions as soon as the spring bulbs can be cleared to make some space. This will make for very big plants that flower earlier than those sown later. With limited space, though, I tend to sow them in early spring and they still flower very well, thriving on being cut weekly for vases. Their role as flowers is to act as airy dancers with enough clout still to compete with the larger blooms of dahlias. Like the dahlias, they bloom until the first hard frost.

OPPOSITE A dense summer combination growing in a large container. The dahlia 'Totally Tangerine' (arguably the best for pots and very profuse in its flowering) is almost being overtaken by annual scabious 'Black Cat' and *Panicum capillare* 'Sparkling Fountain.' The salvia is 'Ember's Wish.' Regular watering is essential for a closely planted summer container, as is picking the vase that will help ensure fresh growth.

BELOW The mulberry pincushion flowers of scabious 'Black Cat' are popular with both wild bumblebees and honeybees alike.

Lilies

The bulbs of oriental and Asiatic lilies resemble curled-up sleeping pangolins, and like these rarest of mammals, lily bulbs are made up of fleshy scales like the head of an artichoke.

Lilies are very happy in pots because they like free-draining soil and, if content, they'll last for decades because the original bulbs will get bigger and multiply. To ensure good flowering for years on end, plant lily bulbs on their own into deep, tall pots using ericaceous compost—this is especially important for the Turk's-cap lilies. Lily bulbs like to be planted quite deeply, at a depth of about 20cm (8 inches). This is because as the central stalks from the bulbs erupt they produce feeding roots before the bud hits the surface of the compost, so the deeper the lily bulb is the more roots it can produce from its stem and the stronger it will grow.

It was the bright red lily beetle, which lays its tiny eggs on the undersides of leaves, that made lilies unpopular for many gardeners, as the awful grub larvae resembles bird shit. But for me, nothing surpasses the glamour of lilies in full bloom! If you haven't already, I urge you to try growing them as not all gardens seem plagued by lily beetles.

ABOVE Tall plastic pots are worth keeping to plant lily bulbs in as they like the depth provided. The Turk's-cap lily *Speciosum* var. *rubrum* 'Uchida' is usually the latest lily to flower.

OPPOSITE A tin bath planted with lily 'Tiger Babies' and 'African Queen.'

Summer seeds to scatter-bomb

Sowing seeds into trays and pots that then need to be pricked out and potted on is a task that to new gardeners can seem both a lot of effort and confusing. Luckily, there are some seeds that can be happily chucked around a small garden, left to simply fall onto the surface of pots and into any nooks and crannies around hard surfaces—it's a great thing to do as a drunken activity! Tip the entire packet of seeds into a jug, then add ten tablespoons of clean sharp sand so that the seeds both scatter more loosely and fall individually, which will allow them to germinate singularly and have a better chance of successfully growing into adult plants.

It's worth noting that some seeds, especially poppies, don't tend to germinate quickly; they often need to experience winter cold before stirring into life. For this reason, store your seed packets in the salad drawer of the

PREVIOUS *Self-seeded hollyhocks in gravel at Chatsworth House (left). Hollyhocks seem to thrive or fail depending on where they are, though they certainly like full sun and can self-seed right into the bases of seemingly bone-dry walls. Self-seeded forget-me-nots flowering from the cracks in bricks (right). Each autumn their descendants will reappear as little hairy rosettes to flower the following spring.*

fridge—this is something that most professional growers do (though on a larger scale, of course) to ensure that their seeds remain virile. The change of temperature experienced by the seeds as they come out of deep cold into the warmth stimulates germination much more quickly.

The best time to direct sow seeds into the disturbed surface soil of pots is in mid-spring (late April in the UK). Seeds that will especially do well by directly sowing include:

✳ calendula ✳ borage ✳ *Linaria maroccana* ✳ hollyhocks ✳ cornflowers ✳ nigella ✳ foxgloves ✳ all poppies ✳ cosmos ✳ Cape daisies ✳ viper's bugloss ✳ *Cerinthe major* ✳ forget-me-nots ✳ honesty ✳ *Phacelia tanacetifolia* ✳ *Erigeron karvinskianus*

Sprinkle these modestly from a height onto pots and window boxes so they land well-spaced out.

OPPOSITE There are many calendulas, or English marigolds, to choose from, however the richest orange is the variety 'Indian Prince' (left). Borage (right) is a large seed that can be direct sown. Once introduced to a garden it will usually self-seed. I prefer to sow it in the summer as it is more attractive as a little seedling than a huge hairy-stemmed being.

BELOW The annual *Linaria maroccana* (left) are effortless to sow directly into cleared and prepared pots, large or small. These are 'Licilia Red' and 'Licilia Violet.' Cornflower 'Black Ball' (right) with bumblebee.

Cardoons. The last episode of *Two Fat Ladies* to be aired, filmed mostly at Woburn Safari Park, sees Clarissa Dickson Wright and Jennifer Paterson come across a walled garden in search of goat cheese. "Beautifully tended by ghosts" Jennifer declares as they march in before Clarissa comes across a clump of her beloved cardoons, a hardy, larger relative of the artichoke that she championed as—in her book at least—edible.

Apparently, the cardoon's young stems can be boiled for an hour to tenderize them and to draw out their bitterness. I don't grow the cardoon for this purpose, but I hope Clarissa would nod at my championing of them at least to be grown. She would have been welcome to come pick some, although doing this sacrifices their flowering, which is the reason I adore them.

These giants of thistles are also known for their beautiful silver-gray leaves, classic characters of William Morris designs that appear in early spring in miniature and swell as spring goes on into summer becoming like huge— but much more elegant—arching umbrella-like beings, a brilliant fountain of leaves. They are an ideal perennial foliage plant to have in the middle of a large pot—be it a large container or terracotta one—permanently and then each winter tulips can be planted around it individually, a few dozen of large varieties such as 'Brown Sugar' and 'Ballerina.' It can be tempting to pick the foliage for the vase but it quickly becomes limp unless it is submerged in cold water overnight beforehand.

From the middle of a cardoon that is over one year old, usually by midsummer, will come the flowering stems of very tight and waxlike sleeping pangolin scales. The flower stem grows tall and steady, reaching 2m (6 feet) if the plant is young and easily 3m (10 feet) once it's mature. The scales open to reveal what becomes, within hours, a complete bee orgy of rich nectar, within a beckoning pool of the most beautiful peacock-neck coloration of both blue and purple. Alas the flowering seems to tire the plant out and so once the bee party is done and the towering beacons fade, cut the whole clump back very hard and then water and mulch the cardoon's pot heavily for the next month; a mulch of well-rotted manure will be welcome. It will be late summer by now usually, but such attention will see the leaves soon resprout and give presence. The old flower stalks with their heads can be stored somewhere to become Christmas decor—wonderful when painted gold—and within the fluff at the base of the heads are sunflower-like seeds. These, if large and firm, will germinate well. Sow them in early spring and the little baby cardoons will grow happily to look like their parents as soon as they grow their first set of proper leaves. If not then you can buy

OPPOSITE 'Brown Sugar' tulips and the rapidly growing leaves of a mature cardoon in a large pot. So that summer annuals, such as cosmos, may be planted here with the resident cardoon, once the tulips have finished they will be lifted out and the entire cardoon will need to be trimmed back, leaving just a few central and emerging leaves to ensure it doesn't smother the annuals while they are small. The faded blooms of cardoons can be dried to be used as winter arrangements, but when they are in bloom the bees will be besotted with them.

OVERLEAF Cardoons and echinops, both hardy perennials, growing together in a raised bed (left) and a cardoon flower that has become a total bee ball (right).

a well-grown 2 liter (3½ pint) potted cardoon plant to place on top of a tulip bulb lasagna in the autumn. If the winter is mild then a few leaves will cling on, giving the pot some stately presence through the season. I used to lift them out with the bulbs once they faded but now I leave them and replant the summer show of dahlias and cosmos around them. If the leaves get too big as these establish then they are just cut off; it does the plant no harm. I like the idea of all my garden's large pots soon having a cardoon within them so the whole place becomes a cardoon jungle.

Runner beans were originally introduced into Europe in the seventeenth century as ornamental plants, and they still have ornamental value despite becoming more recognized as members of the kitchen garden. I especially like to grow the pink runner bean that is 'Aurora' up maroon-flowering sunflowers—the pink bubble gum-bean flower with such a different and

LEFT The runner bean 'Aurora' growing up the stem of sunflower 'Claret.' The runner bean needs to be sown after the sunflower has been planted out into its final large pot. This is so that the sunflower's stem gets a good month of growing as a head start before it becomes the runner bean's climbing frame.

OPPOSITE A pot in the kitchen garden at Chatsworth House staked with little twigs for the dwarf runner bean variety 'Jackpot.'

surprisingly delicate form, almost like a tiny orchid, is an attention-grabbing partner against the big face of the claret sunflower. You can direct sow the runner bean seeds under the sunflower seedlings once they have started to romp away and have grown a good eight pairs of leaves. For a Medusa-like mass of falling and crazed runner bean flowers that won't tower over the pots, direct sow between three and five seeds of the dwarf runner bean that is 'Jackpot.' Runner beans are especially hungry plants, so they will flourish in a rich mix of compost and well-rotted manure. Tear up old toilet-roll tubes and place these in the bottom of the pot, as they will hold on to moisture for the roots to absorb more easily in the heat of the summer.

Pumpkins are even hungrier than runner beans and if you don't grow your own 'Crown Prince' you'll regret not having the most stylish of still-life adornments for All Hallows' Eve. Just sow one seed as the plant will need its own large pot to romp away in—a pumpkin late sown in the first week of June (early summer) is often a good succession to sweet peas as they fade out in the early summer heat, and the seedling will be chomping at the bit to get going just as the last of the sweet peas are cut down. A pumpkin will enjoy growing up the wigwam that they once adorned, and the plant's leaves are wonderfully characterful. In the evenings, mist the foliage with liquid seaweed feed to prevent it getting mildewy too quickly. The flowers of pumpkins are

ABOVE The sunflower 'Earthwalker' has variable flowers of orange to scarlet—some large, some small—making it a very good cut flower variety.

OPPOSITE The huge, dinner-plate-sized, sunshine faces of sunflowers, typically grown in childhood classrooms, rarely fail to raise a smile. Once they have finished flowering you have a huge seedhead to use as a bird feeder or a treat to hang up for chickens to peck at.

wonderful, too, being open to say hello to you in the mornings and looking very happy to be alive with a bumblebee eagerly visiting them. Most of these blooms will be males, but one or two precious female ones will have the start of a swelling fruit at their flower bases.

FIGS

On the bank of the River Thames, I think quite near the home of the Chelsea Flower Show, is the most wonderful mop-headed, umbrella-like fig tree; it looks like it's drunk and tipping into the river, and you see London's ring-necked parakeets flocking out and into it, screaming thrillingly. Figs today are one of my go-to small trees for a sunny pot garden. I love everything about them, from their wonderful rounded-edged leaves to their smooth, whirling trunks in the winter. The only sad thing is they don't blossom—at least not to our eyes. The blossom is in fact internal, located within the tiny fruits, and these are either self-fertile or rely on a minuscule fig wasp to crawl in and pollinate them. Ever since Dame Judi Dench opened a video for the Woodland Trust saying, "Now, I'd like you to meet Mr. Fig," I've really fallen for figs, and they are very happy to grow in pots. They fruit best if they feel quite pot-bound, but should be grown in dustbin-sized pots to give them stature.

🌱 THERE ARE SOME BRILLIANT FIG NAMES...

* 'Little Miss Figgy' – A dwarf cultivar of the traditional variety 'Violette de Bordeaux,' producing sweet golden-skinned figs and has an especially attractive bushy habit.

* 'Rouge de Bordeaux' – The most alluring fruit, ripening like a dark plum with a deep red flesh.

* 'Sultane' – Very sweet, often grown commercially as it is particularly fast growing, becoming a heavy-cropping tree within a few seasons.

* 'Panachee' – An exotic tiger fig with stripy, strawberry-tasting fruits.

* 'Doree' – Renowned as a heavy-cropping fig tree with a helpfully compact growing habit and large fruits.

It is advisable, though, if planting newly bought 2- or 3-liter (3½–5 pint) potted figs, to place them first into what are sinisterly called root-control bags and then plant them centrally in their new large pots. These bags encourage fibrous roots; when the root tips meet the sides of the bag their apical dominance is interrupted, and helpful new feeder (fibrous) roots develop. This prevents roots from circling the pot and enables better absorption of water and nutrients by the fig. The restrictive stress of this approach surprisingly causes them to fruit better than if they are planted into rich soil, which results in vigorous house-scaling growth but little fruit production. They do need full sun, though, to flourish. There are some brilliant names for fig varieties, besides the common 'Brown Turkey' fig (see the box opposite).

Fig leaves – Despite their rough texture, fig leaves become surprisingly delicate when pressed, almost like tracing paper. Pick the leaves on a dry day and then press each leaf within a sandwich of two blotting-paper sheets within either a large flower press or a large book. Inspect them every few days; as they are very delicate, not all will survive their transformation. Those that make it after three weeks of being pressed can be painted or sprayed golden for Christmas—they'll look incredible (see page 182).

ABOVE The picking test for figs should be done on a sunny day. You will know that the fig is ready when its small stem attached to the main branch begins to droop down. A little droplet of sugar may also be produced at the bottom of the ripened, purple fruit.

HERBS

Herbs are heaven sent for pots, and in sunny, small gardens they should make up a very high percentage of what is being grown—especially if the gardener is short on time, because if herbs have good drainage and sun they will flourish on the neglect that they originated in and will fill the air with fragrance. Scent is a powerful mood enhancer, and if you can dive-bomb your nose into something organic and scented you can shut out everything for a few moments. Herbs are close to being nature's equivalent of amyl nitrite poppers, and although they may not be able to get you heedlessly dancing, they can help to take the edge off a bad day!

When visiting pubs that serve food, I always think it a positive sign if they have a lot of herbs growing in the parking lot or around the outdoor tables, as any good chef will want to be able to go and pick proper fresh herbs rather than use imported stems in plastic bags. It's bonkers that even the hardy herbs for sale in our supermarkets, such as rosemary, are flown in from Portugal and beyond, and so carry a massive number of air miles, when we could have fields of such crops here all the year-round.

The traditional hardy herbs that are stalwarts of the kitchen garden are pretty much foolproof and will survive year-round in pots if placed in sunny positions. All herbs, in fact, aside from the shrub-like interloper that is the bay tree, will sulk in the shade. They like to be on the dry side of life, growing very well in poor soils. Herbs, therefore, fall into the category of plants that make a good choice for the garden novice, but what often kills them is overwatering, as they don't like to be waterlogged at all, so drainage holes are especially vital. The compost can be of poor quality if that's all you have, but try to combine it with some good molehill soil to liven it up, and mix in any grit that you have generously to further aid drainage and fool their roots into feeling they are growing in their native gritty and sandy Mediterranean terrain.

Should you not be a devoted cook who trims the plants each week, herbs still earn their place in the garden, because their flowers are very rich in nectar, making them fantastic pollinator magnets, too, not to mention their scented leaves whose flavors are almost always richer when freshly picked as and when you need them.

ABOVE, TOP Lavender is rightfully known as the bee provider, and the traditional varieties 'Hidcote' and 'Gros Bleu' have the richest nectar provisions. Sharp drainage and full sun are essential.

ABOVE, BOTTOM Fennel in pots, swaying their tall, wind-resistant seedheads along a London street. I'd be glad of a garden full of self-seeded fennel as it's a beautiful foil for tulips.

OPPOSITE My friend Fran's dolphin (or possibly koi carp) statue in the middle of a shallow birdbath among lavender. The water will be welcomed by honeybees as they can easily land on the birdbath's wide rim.

Rosemary is a hardy herb that wins the day for me in terms of having at least one plant in the garden for winter's frost to settle on. It seems to indulge in the darkness of winter, standing emerald and stoic, and its dark green, busy turrets are something you will be very thankful for. The rule is to not cut back into its hard wood because if you do then the frost will get into the heart of it, which can kill it, especially if it is a young plant. Gentle trimmings for the kitchen will do no harm, but coppice-like cutting can be fatal. Hard pruning of leggy plants should only be done in late spring and early summer, when frosts are over, and only where shoots are visible—any lower and you risk shocking the plant into an early death. Essentially you want to give them a decent haircut to encourage good bushiness.

Lavender is also hardy but more problematic when it comes to pruning as its seedheads are a favorite of goldfinches. Traditionally, it is cut back as soon as its purple flowers fade to gray in late summer, taking the stems and about 2.5cm (1 inch) of the foliage off with shears to encourage the plant to be bushy. If you are keen on using the dried flowers in lavender bags, say, you'll still want to do this. Alternatively, you can leave the bushes intact for the flowers to dry on the plant so goldfinches can feed on them over the winter, in which case you should give the bushes a prune in late spring (May in the UK).

Mint is treated differently to other herbs as it thrives on producing fresh, tender, soft growth each year rather than forming any woody stems. What happens to it often in pots, though, is that it goes crazy in its first year but then seems to lose its gusto and sends up just a few weedy stems in its second season. This means the roots need to be stimulated to encourage more youthful growth. To do this, tip the tired mint out of its pot and take a bread knife to the root ball, cutting it up so each bit of its white roots is trimmed to a length of about 10cm (4 inches) and they have the appearance of a load of snipped-up spaghetti! You then simply tip the entire cut-up root ball back into its original pot, mix it in with the old compost, and just dress the top of the pot with some fresh compost. Within three weeks you should see fresh, vigorous spurs of mint pushing up.

Mints are a wonderful choice for a sunny window box; they come in an incredible variety of wonderful scents and leaf colors, and if not cut back too much, their flowers will welcome in bees of many species. The key to keeping the essence of individual mint scents is to grow only one variety per pot. Mint makes a brilliant cut foliage, too—and why not, given its perfumed virtues.

OPPOSITE Lavender planted into a thin trench of earth right under a wall, along a sunny village road (above left). Sage in flower (above right). Marjoram (below left) and strawberry mint (below right) being visited by bees.

ABOVE Rosemary is an especially valuable herb for bees as it flowers in late winter and can create a brilliant hedge for sunny and dry places.

Lemon verbena is the most fragrant of herbs and its tea-making attributes surpass even those of mint. From a little, woody, twiglike framework, willowlike leaves sprout and grow throughout the summer. These leaves are of an especially beautiful, sweet lemon scent, which is noticeable as you brush your hands through it. In a sunny, protected garden it is worth planting it into the ground where, if the location is to its liking, the plant will grow during the summer to a wonderful size, much more so than it will do in a pot, though it will still be content in a container nonetheless.

The bigger the verbena can become the better, because this will result in more of its leaves being produced, which can then be picked and used to make the most refreshing and divinely perfumed of teas. If you pick the leaves every week throughout the summer and dry them, the tea will be even more flavorsome. I'd have lots of lemon verbena plants if space allowed because I struggle to find the leaves to buy as a dried tea. The last harvest of leaves is therefore precious and it's a sad late-winter's day when the jar of verbena leaves is found to be empty. For two mugs of tea, I place half a dozen leaves or a sprig in the lobster-claw-like tongs of an antique tea infuser, pour over boiling water, and leave to infuse in the mug for a few minutes.

The little shrub-like herb will need protection during the cold and wet of the winter, understandably, as it is native to South America. By late autumn, or whenever the first hard frost is forecast, any grown in pots will need to be moved indoors. Those in the ground against sunny walls will appreciate a good mulch around them of leaves or old compost. The summer's growth of twigs should all be pruned back to the thick central stump, with each last leaf picked off and savored. The verbena will not need to be watered but it should be kept in a cold but frost-free place until it can be woken up again in late spring (May in the UK). At this time, give the plant a little water and scrape away 5cm (2 inches) of the old surface compost and replace it with a mulch of fresh compost. From the seemingly dead stump, fresh little shoots should spur into growth as the weather warms. I have two such verbena plants that reign supreme as statement pot plants through the summer because of their elegant shape, despite them having little in the way of flowers (these are tiny and white). The leaves are of a zesty green and are picked for tea almost like cut-and-come-again salad leaves. Plants will flourish when regularly picked and with weekly watering throughout the summer.

OPPOSITE Lemon verbena's flowers are nothing to write home about, but its leaves, when turned into a tea, are truly heaven sent and are considered an antioxidant.

Autumn

Carnival time, the light at its very diamond-cutting best making dahlia faces appear as sea creatures and the seedheads of grasses shimmer like glittering witchcraft. On the last golden days, sit and absorb the sun's rays and the birdsong. If the summer has been especially hot then now will be a time for the birds to find some sanctuary as wet dawns help to soften the soil, bringing worms to its surface. It is abundance time for dahlia picking and everything should be allowed to tumble and dance into each other; don't rush the season on.

Fallen and fermenting plums in the autumn sun will see the red admiral butterflies flutter down to become drunk as they sip the juice. These bold and large butterflies were in medieval times considered to be so bizarrely sinister in their coloration that they were often referred to as the devil's fly! Like the similar-in-size peacock butterflies, they require nettles for their caterpillars but they also sometimes lay eggs on hops (*Humulus lupulus*).

Opposite: Two varieties—'September Ruby' and 'Violetta'—of hardy perennial New England aster. They glow with nectar, beckoning in all bees and butterflies.

The good grasses

You need to be careful with grasses in pots, especially perennial ones, because all too quickly the flame-gun-like browned and vanilla clumps that many varieties have all the year round can create the impression of a Wild West film set, scattered with tumbleweed. Not so, though, with the lush green foliage of the *Chasmanthium latifolium*, otherwise known as the rolled oats grass, a common name that does little to truly complement its fish-scale-like flat seedheads that shimmer like polished copper pennies in the wind. Some nurseries also refer to it sweetly as the mini bamboo. In a pot where it isn't disturbed by others it will earn a permanent place, with its blades fading from green to an autumnal mix of yellow and then browns in the winter. In spring the foliage can be cut back to the clump's base and fresh growth will spur up. From the age of two, though, this perennial grass becomes the peacock of its kin due to its fishing-rod-like seedheads that display elegantly out of the clump, arching and dancing. You can pick the seedheads for a dried vase inside and they'll look beautiful for months if not years afterward. If you are growing this grass from seed you need patience, as it can often take upward of almost two months to begin germination.

The second grass that I love and plant with everything due to its champagne-like-fizz seedheads is *Panicum capillare* 'Sparkling Fountain.' If this most beautiful of plants decides to like your garden it should self-seed wonderfully. It partners well with most things because it's very happy-go-lucky and doesn't take energy from thirstier and hungrier plants. It is an annual, so if it doesn't self-seed you need to sow it once a year. The seed is annoyingly tiny and needs light to germinate, so sprinkle it into a small seed tray and prick out the seedlings when they are well grown.

OPPOSITE *Panicum capillare* 'Sparkling Fountain' gives pots a magical sparkle over the summer and autumn. It is not a greedy annual, and therefore a good partner for dahlias in pots.

ABOVE, TOP Once the perennial *Chasmanthium latifolium* is three years old it will have clumped up well and provided many seed stems. It's a plant for a permanent pot and ideal for a windy terrace.

ABOVE, BOTTOM The annual millet 'Red Jewel.' Grow it together with the larger variety 'Violaceum,' or combine with cosmos.

Dahlias

Believe it or not, when it comes to dahlias, my mantra is now less is more! Why and how can such a change in attitude have arisen? As with spring tulips, I used to cram them into every possible pot, but this meant a lot of potting up, feeding, staking, and watering and, to be honest, when it comes to flower performance and cutting plants in pots, cosmos outdo dahlias by quite a mile. Dahlias can be divas in pots. They hate wind and exposed places, they can rot if they are overwatered but will stall and get mildew if they are underwatered and underfed. The hot summer of 2022 saw dahlias in many British gardens fail badly, with flowering recovering for only a few weeks in the cool of late autumn.

So I now restrict myself to about nine to twelve dahlias a year, which is a big reduction considering I once grew about thirty! Of these, the majority will be the single Bishop or anemone-flowering varieties, because I find that these prosper far better as well as look better in pots than the big decorative types, which often have large, cabbage-like leaves. The Bishops especially have attractive dark foliage, lacy like that of a black elder or even an acer, and they are prolific in their simple but stained-glass colored flowers that pollinators adore. Larger in size and duller in its foliage is the purple butterfly-attracting 'Blue Bayou,' while of a perfect size for pots, reaching some 50cm (20 inches), is 'Totally Tangerine.' Of the decorative dahlias, my favorite is the huge, junglelike 'Black Jack.' A glossy giant of dark leaves and enormous sea urchin flowers, it will grow like a weed but, alas, can be late to flower compared to others, so in some respects its more traditional cousin, 'Rip City,' wins its class. In terms of giving prolific and long-lasting cut flowers, 'Molly Raven' is the best, with antique, smoky silklike petals.

Pot up dahlias in late spring, because if you do it any earlier and are without a greenhouse it is impractical, space-wise, to start them off indoors. Each tuber should be placed into a 2 or 3 liter (3½ or 5 pint) pot. Fill the pot almost to the top with compost, then place the tuber in the center, covering it over so that there is little more than 2.5cm (1 inch) of compost on top. This is important, as the tuber needs to feel the warmth near the surface of the soil to help stir it into growth. Lightly water the freshly potted-up tubers, increasing the amount as the dahlias sprout—bear in mind that too much water will cause the tubers to rot. Each night, cover over the potted tubers with burlap bags to protect them from any cold nights, and if a frost is

PREVIOUS *Salvia × jamensis* and salvia 'Love and Wishes' growing with *Panicum capillare* 'Sparkling Fountain' in the gulley of a wall, acting like a long window box, in dappled shade.

ABOVE Dahlia 'Molly Raven' is a very prolific, beautiful dahlia for a large pot.

OPPOSITE Choosing dahlias with cut flowers in mind allows a circus to come to town. I have used vintage bud vases here. They have a brilliantly helpful base weight. Left, top to bottom, are 'Autumn Orange,' 'Tartan,' and 'Molly Raven.' Middle, top to bottom, are 'Thomas A. Edison,' 'Jowey Joshua,' 'Brown Sugar,' and 'Verrone's Obsidian' (the only one here that is pollinator friendly). On the right are 'Hans Auinger' (bottom) and 'Mats' (top).

forecast your dahlia crop will need to be taken inside for the night! Dahlias dislike being overcrowded, so the more room each plant has in its container, the better it will grow, which is why I now plant only one dahlia per large container or dustbin. If the growth tips are pinched out once six pairs of leaves have grown, this will cause each plant to bush up incredibly well and more flowers will be produced, too. When the dahlias are young, slugs are the biggest threat, so place the growing plants on tables to reduce the risk of being nibbled. Picking and deadheading of the flowers is essential, as dahlias thrive on feeling that they must produce fresh growth, so be bold and cut stems down into the heart of the plant, always to a pair of leaves, as from such junctions fresh buds will erupt surprisingly quickly.

Once the dahlias begin to romp they will need staking, either with a few sticks of branchy silver birch that will create a clawlike cage or use several bamboo canes, tying each stem of the dahlia to them in a figure of eight. Whatever you use, take care not to push down the stakes too near the dahlia itself, to avoid fatally stabbing through the tuber. Dahlias go wonderfully well with *Panicum capillare* 'Sparkling Fountain' as an under and upper story of fluff, and thunbergias will happily use dahlia stems as climbing frames.

When it comes to storing dahlias for the winter months, the tubers need to be put to bed dry, not wet, as it's damp that causes the fungal spores that rot the tuber. I tend to stop watering my dahlias in late autumn, around All Hallows' Eve, then lift the tubers from the pots two weeks later, crumbling and brushing off as much soil as I can. Then I spread them all out on newspaper under the kitchen table for a few nights to help them dry out properly. Once dry to the touch, and I've checked they are all firm, they are each wrapped in newspaper, placed in a thick cardboard box, and stored. The best place for storing is an unheated spare room, or a garden shed, provided the shed is not damp! If you want to keep track of what each of your dahlia varieties is, attach a luggage label with the dahlia's name on it to the thickest stem, as once you have cut off the foliage and lifted the tubers they will all look similar.

OPPOSITE A favorite pairing of nectar-rich and bee-friendly dahlias of good heights, the tall, claret 'Bishop of Auckland' and the shorter nectarine punch of 'Waltzing Mathilda.' Both are growing in a dolly tub.

ABOVE Dahlia 'Black Jack' has a wonderful dark green, junglelike foliage that easily grows to 1.5m (5 feet). Alas it often doesn't flower until autumn rather than in summer. It is worth the wait, however, with staking certainly required.

CLOCKWISE FROM TOP LEFT Good dahlias for pollinators. 'Bishop of York' is best picked after a few days as the buttercup yellow becomes too lemon. 'Verrone's Obsidian' is like a shooting star. 'Blue Bayou' is not blue but sugar-plum purple and wonderfully exotic. It grows quite tall and is beloved of butterflies. 'Totally Tangerine' is one of the best varieties for pots, which don't have to be huge in size. 'Bishop of Canterbury' is a deep cerise pink and 'Sarah Raven' looks as if made of strawberry jam. The seed-grown single dahlia 'Bishop's Children' will flower with gusto just a few months after being sown.

Pelargoniums

Pelargoniums don't seem to like me. Ignorantly, I didn't much like them either until a few years ago, snobbishly lumping them with the happy-go-lucky bedding geraniums that are pelargoniums' close and often misidentified cousins. What distinguishes pelargoniums from geraniums is their flower petals, the latter having five petals that are all identical and the former having two upper petals that slightly differ from the three lower ones.

No matter, I am impressed with even bedding geraniums now, not really as bedding plants but as cut flowers, for if they are picked they have an incredible vase life, looking good for a week at least, often longer. So if I am without any flowers in my own garden, I am often tempted to do some "live" deadheading from roundabouts or from one of my neighbors' pots because they don't deadhead their pelargoniums at all and are often away for weeks, so it in fact does everyone concerned a favor!

As I write this, I am on a train to Nottingham with a small pot that carries a healthy-looking little species of pelargonium that I bought at a plant sale a week ago. It has an incredibly strong stem dancing around as if it's made from a sturdy piece of fishing line. This surprising and ethereal strength is proven here as it's been peeking confidently out of the top of my burlap bags. I've carried it in on a journey that's involved a taxi, train, and bus, with some hasty walking in between. Its flowers are small for a pelargonium, but they are delicately beautiful, each one being a bursting star of dark mulberry-jam coloration, the petals curving gently outward. The small, round, and crinkly edged leaves have a beautiful velvety texture and are of a rich ocean-green complexion, although in certain light you'd be forgiven for declaring them dull. I am hopeful that my mum has more success in nurturing this little one than I have had. Mum hasn't really commented on it yet, but that's not surprising as it's one of those plants that reveals its exotic splendor in the right light.

I got very excited one spring and ordered several rooted pelargoniums from the incredible Fibrex, a dedicated nursery that is sadly no longer but once had one of the largest collections of these flowers. I chose bright and dark-flowering Regals that look like frilly faced dragons with fabulous names to match their looks—titles abound here, enough lords and ladies, earls and countesses to fill the pages of *Country Life* magazine tenfold.

OPPOSITE The classiest pelargonium of all is 'Attar of Roses.' If its growth tips are pinched out, stopping it from getting tall, it will bush up beautifully within a month and jelly out of a pot marvelously. Young first- and second-year plants usually flower better than older ones but its flowers are not its trump card, its perfumed leaves are. A pot such as this will need to be moved to somewhere frost free—usually indoors—in most regions for it to survive the increasingly cold winters.

ABOVE The pelargonium 'Prince of Orange' will seem an odd title until its foliage is smelled! It grows well in small tabletop pots.

All of them, though, hated being indoors. Rather than being easy, I found them needy and unhappy at their indoor residence; leaves became yellow and fell off, while aphids gathered at their tips. The only group of pelargoniums that I have had success with and love for their vigor are the scented-leaf varieties 'Attar of Roses,' which smells of Turkish delight, and 'Prince of Orange,' which smells of citrus but carries a bright pink flower rather than an orange one. 'Attar of Roses' is especially frost hardy in a city microclimate, provided its summer growth isn't cut back until late spring (late May in the UK), as when left on it will protect the plant's crown. They can both, though, be treated as houseplants for the winter in a cold room. In such situations, be sure to water them lightly every fortnight.

Scented pelargoniums are good as indoor houseplants as they seem to resist aphid infestations, perhaps due to their fragrance, but it's still well worth regularly inspecting them and removing any leaves that are found to be harboring colonies. For an incredibly perfumed bathroom, place some scented pelargonium leaves in a muslin bag under a running tap of hot water! The plants can go back outside by late spring (May in the UK). A seaweed feed from then onward will be beneficial. The grooming of pelargoniums is required often as they hold onto their dried and dead leaves.

I take cuttings of these pelargoniums because the younger plants are more vigorous than the parents; these seem to lose their flowering gusto once they

FAR LEFT Delicate and exotic-looking *Pelargonium sidoides*.

LEFT A terracotta pot of pelargonium cuttings on the windowsill, where they will feel warmer and so hopefully root quickly. All but two leaves on each cutting have been taken off to aid rooting.

get to about three years old, but this isn't a problem really as the foliage is the main attraction. Pinching out the growth tips little and often, or cutting the stems for the vase will ensure that large plants remain bushy rather than leggy, which is important for the overall look of the plant.

However, 'Attar of Roses' especially is the easiest thing to propagate from midsummer into early autumn. The key thing to be aware of when taking a pelargonium cutting is that on each part of the stem where there is a pair of leaves is a knuckle like the ones on your finger, known as a node, and it is from these nodes that roots can sprout once the stem is pushed into some soil. From the top growth tip of the chosen pelargonium stem, count down to three pairs of leaves. Cut just under the third pair of leaves and then strip off these and the leaves above it, apart from the top pair at the top of the cutting. The last thing to do is to pinch off the growth tip so that the cutting has only one or two leaves left at the top. The growth tip will often be small, in between the remaining pair of leaves. You pinch out this so that the cutting cannot think about growing anything other than its roots. Although this sounds barbarous, it will give the cutting the best chance of growing because the stress of it transpiring (losing water) has been hugely reduced, and the one or two leaves left on will still allow the plant to photosynthesize enough.

Take six cuttings at a time, as not all of them will manage to root. Push each one around the sides of a small 9cm (3½ inch) plastic or terracotta pot that has been filled to the brim with gritty multipurpose compost, as the sides are warmer and therefore will encourage the cuttings to root faster. The pot of cuttings should be placed on a sunny windowsill, but you don't need to put a plastic bag over them, just make sure the pot doesn't dry out by lightly watering once a week. Any cuttings that droop and die should be removed, but avoid disturbing the other cuttings until you see a few roots coming out of the bottom of the pot. When you do, pot up each cutting individually.

ABOVE A welcome jolly vase of typical bedding geraniums that last brilliantly well as cut flowers. The cutting of their flowers will, just like with cosmos, encourage more blooms to be produced.

Winter

The often-demonized season can be forgiven, as although the cold and slumbering it brings is at times brutal, it makes the spring a season to be longed for and loved all the more. The microclimates of city and walled gardens will see such little gardens envied by those with large ones in the countryside, as smaller gardens will nurture plants that are considered to be tender during especially cold and freezing nights. Winters are becoming windier, colder, and overall, it seems, drier, with rain flooding over a few hours rather than gently drizzling. So the watering of pots containing bulbs may be required little and often.

Many butterflies hibernate through the winter, including the peacock butterfly, which is arguably the prettiest of all butterflies. The eyelike markings are used to try and scare away predators such as mice, which prove especially troublesome to sleeping butterflies during their winter's sleep. Its caterpillars hatch over the summer, feed as a herd once they have hatched out, spinning a protective weblike cloak around themselves as they move through clumps of nettles in an attempt at deterring predatory wasps.

Opposite: A male blackbird, pecking an apple placed among geums on a winter's morning.

Crab apples

In spring, crab apples blossom with gusto to the delight of bees and then, from early autumn into late winter, their fruits resemble Christmas tree decorations. The colder the winter days get the more appealing and sweeter in flavor the fruits become to songbirds, especially blackbirds. You can also, of course, make crab apple jelly with these fruits, and I love to have a few whole crab apples to wire into a Christmas wreath.

Like roses, crab apple trees are best planted during the winter when a larger variety of them will be available as dormant bare-root trees. A crab apple tree will want a decent-sized pot—either of a large container or old dustbin size. The crab apples will then need to be watered once a week from mid-spring (April in the UK) onward for them to blossom and fruit well, and they will benefit from a good 10cm (4 inch) mulch with well-rotted organic manure in the spring.

🌱 MY FAVORITE VARIETIES ARE

* 'Evereste' – Scarlet flower buds open to white spring blossom with red, yellow, and orange-blushed marbled fruits. It can reach 7m (22 feet) tall with a conically shaped crown.

* 'Gorgeous' – Similar to 'Evereste' and said to be the best for crab apple jelly.

* 'Wisley Crab' – The largest crab apple, it looks like a *Snow White* pantomime prop when in blossom. The fruits are so large that they all drop off once the autumnal winds properly set in, and as tempting as the shining blood-red apples look, they are incredibly tart.

* 'Indian Magic' – Deep-pink blossom and a broadly shaped tree, the fruits are small but abundant, looking like bohemian Christmas fairy lights.

* 'Scarlett' – Similar to 'Indian Magic,' with an impressive orange leaf color in the autumn.

Hellebores

Let no roses aside from those of the winter-flowering Christmas roses be seen during the winter, least of all for Valentine's Day!

For those with shady pot gardens, it is in winter and spring that hellebores can truly take dark and dank places by storm. Exhibiting a hardy sophistication as if they were dahlias, they have an air of witchcraft and Narnia's Snow Queen about them. Their pollen-laden faces will be a welcome feast for any freshly awakened queen bumblebees.

A great deal of breeding has been put into hellebores lately, so that you can have varieties such as 'Maestro' that begin their flowering season in early winter (December in the UK), followed by 'Merlin,' which starts to flower in mid-winter (late January in the UK). Onward from here the color can get into more pink, scarlet, and even navy, almost black, thanks to the *Helleborus × hybridus* varieties. The sturdiest, tallest, and most upright of the lot, though, is the Corsican hellebore; it gets on with life almost anywhere and it's freshly cut, lime green flowers are very welcome in the gray days of mid-winter.

All hellebores are an investment in terms of price, because when you buy a plant that's in flower it is likely to be around three years of age—that's a long time for a nursery to have raised a plant for before it's large enough to sell in good flower. However, they are perennials, returning each year, which makes the cost worthwhile.

Hellebores make excellent cut flowers, but the secret to them being good in the vase is once they have been cut to totally submerge them—their flowers, stems, leaves, and all—overnight in a sink of cold water. They will naturally float so place a flannel on top of them to help the cold water properly wet them. In the morning, select their vases and then cut them to length, then sear their stem ends in boiling water for fifteen seconds before arranging them into the filled vases of cold water straight away. If you don't do this they'll go limp and will be a complete waste! Searing confuses people easily: it's just the last inch of the stem ends that are to be zapped by the boiling water, hold the flowers out of the steam as you do so, then plunge the stems immediately into cold water.

For the rest of the year their deep green evergreen leaves will give sturdy presence in a shady corner surrounded by ferns and hostas, provided they aren't allowed to dry out.

ABOVE, TOP *Helleborus × hybridus* Harvington red. These hellebores readily cross-pollinate and are easy to grow from seed, resulting in an array of colors.

ABOVE, BOTTOM The waxlike flower of the tough Corsican hellebore. It makes a real statement from mid-winter to early spring with a large, clustering stem of flowers.

OPPOSITE Recent breeding of hellebores has seen some varieties flower earlier in the winter, often just after Christmas. These include 'Merlin' and 'Maestro' (pictured here).

Amaryllis

I'm not a houseplant person, but I have a soft spot for amaryllis, perhaps because of the clout of these bulbs. Conditioned to swell and flower in their first season, the bulbs send up the most dramatic giraffes of stems that open into huge wonderland-like beings at a time when the outside weather is often so miserable.

The effort begins once the flowers are over. Amaryllis have fleshy roots and love to feel pot-bound and snug, like agapanthus. Once their flowers have faded the long flower stem can be cut off, right down completely, but their strappy leaves need to be left in situ. Clean these with the inside of a banana skin now and then and feed the bulb (which should have been planted half poking out of the soil's surface) with liquid seaweed fortnightly. By summer, the bulb will have grown several long, scrappy, quite untidy leaves and so provides little indoor-worthy interest. Now that the weather is warm they can be placed outside—what would be more ideal though, if you or a friend has one, is to put them in a greenhouse over the summer as the bulb will enjoy the high temperatures that will be felt under glass. But wherever it is, don't neglect it—continue to feed and water it until the autumn, when you can cease this and let the leaves become limp and frazzled. Some people recommend then placing them in the dark for two months at this point, an unlit garage or shed, for example. Once the leaves have crinkled up you can cut them off and, nearer to Christmas, you can bring the pot back inside. Start to water the plant, always around the edge of the bulb; a mug's worth weekly. Once it senses the moisture and heat of being indoors you should see it begin to reshoot. Sometimes indoor pots containing the likes of amaryllis become plagued with little black fruit-like flies, known properly as sciarid flies. The way to keep these at bay is to dress the surface of the compost generously with cinnamon powder to the point that the surface looks like very bad fake tan generously sprinkled onto burned toast.

Will it flower in time for Christmas or New Year as willingly as a freshly bought bulb? Probably not. Annoyingly, amaryllis seem to enjoy playing the guessing game and they will frequently flower at a time of their choosing, rather than ours, but whenever they do so an amaryllis flower is a lovely thing.

OPPOSITE Amaryllis 'Green Magic' tower like giraffes among overwintering pelargoniums on the windowsill. The display requires weekly watering due to central heating.

ABOVE, TOP Known as the butterfly amaryllis, Papillo will often be more expensive than more cultivated varieties but it is arguably the most exotic and resplendent.

ABOVE, BOTTOM Amaryllis 'Mandela' is a real morello-cherry red. It seems to take the longest to flower from when its bulbs are planted.

OPPOSITE Pressed fig leaves sprayed gold are beautiful for Christmas.
ABOVE Pressed viola 'Tigers Eye' varieties glued delicately to Christmas cards. I use the craft glue Mod Podge.

Planting lists

Here's my list for perennial-plant shopping, for a scented, exuberant, but low-maintenance pot garden, such as a sunny and exposed city balcony belonging to someone who might get into the habit of watering their pots once a week—or indeed less—during the summer. All these would do well on a roof garden, too. If an automatic irrigation system can be put in place so much the better, as this list is more for permanent, perennial planting than temporary color.

* Agapanthus – For form and flowers; the seedheads can be left on for winter structure.
* Figs – For canopies. Think of them as natural garden umbrellas, placing their pots near a garden table.
* Rosemary – For hedging and winter structure, culinary use, scent, and to attract bees.
* Sage and thyme – For culinary use, scent, and to attract bees.
* *Alchemilla mollis* – For zaps of acid-green and fluffy flowerlike foliage; wonderful picked for display. Cut back plants often to keep them looking fresh.
* Lavender – For winter form, scent, and to attract bees and finches.
* Buddleia Buzz Series – For scent and to attract bees.
* *Verbena bonariensis* – For prolific flowers and airy height; to attract bees, butterflies, and moths, plus blue tits and finches especially like the seedheads.
* Bay – For winter structure and culinary use.
* Cardoon/artichoke – For form and flowers, old flower stems provide winter structure or can be harvested for indoor decoration at Christmas. Especially attractive to bees and butterflies when in flower.
* *Chasmanthium latifolium* – For form and seedheads, which can be harvested as dried decorations.
* *Eucalyptus nicholii* – For form, an airy and evergreen small tree or bush if cut back each year in late spring.
* Lemon verbena – For wonderful scent, structural pot plant, and a wonderful tea.
* Mint – For scent, to attract bees, and culinary use (good in cocktails).
* Scented leaf pelargoniums – 'Attar of Roses' has Turkish-delight-scented leaves, and is stylish and unusual.
* *Dierama pulcherrimum* or angel's fishing rod – Flowering perennial of arching, wirelike flower stems.
* *Eryngium giganteum* 'Miss Willmott's Ghost' – A short-lived perennial that may self-seed, for incredible winter seedheads.
* Seeds that are worth scattering about – *Panicum capillare* 'Sparkling Fountain,' honesty, calendula, linaria, *Cerinthe major*. Foxgloves, poppies, and viper's bugloss will all happily self-seed into nooks and crannies and pop up each year.
* Perennial bulbs to add – Crocus, *Iris reticulata*, narcissi, and alliums. Plant once and these will return each spring.

OPPOSITE Troughs of permanently planted agapanthus and lavender. They are ideal for sunny and exposed situations but they will still appreciate and need some watering during the heat of summer.

My list for a shady balcony or basement garden, belonging to someone who might get into the habit of watering their pots once a week during the summer months. Hardy plants that provide foliage take over largely from flowers here.

* Ferns – *Athyrium niponicum* var. *pictum* 'Metallicum,' *Matteuccia struthiopteris*.
* Japanese acers.
* Hostas.
* Hellebores 'Merlin' and Maestro' and *Helleborus argutifolius*, the holly-leafed hellebore.
* Bay.
* Holly – As either standard or bush but buy in the berry to be sure of having a decorative female!
* Ivy – Ideal for growing in pots up permanent metal tepees where it can be easily kept in check.
* *Mahonia eurybracteata* 'Soft Caress.'
* *Hydrangea anomala* subsp. *petiolaris* – Useful self-clinging climber for walls.
* *Acanthus mollis*, bear's breeches, 'Rue Lodan.'
* Seeds that are worth scattering about – Nicotiana and foxgloves.
* Spring-flowering bulbs to add – Snowdrops, *Cyclamen coum*, crocus, *Iris reticulata*, aconites, and hyacinths.

BELOW Nicotiana will be happy in shade over the summer. Nicotiana 'Lime Green' (left) planted with the red nicotiana 'Baby Bella' (right).

OPPOSITE Hostas and ferns provide dramatic leaves and a sense of green calm in shady places such as porches or sunken gardens.

It takes a few seasons to get into the rhythm of your garden jobs, but this guide should assist in at least getting the essential jobs done to ensure each season has some pizzazz to it.

LATE WINTER

* Sow sweet pea seeds and *Cobaea scandens*. The latter needs to be sown on a warm windowsill and kept inside until early summer (June in the UK).

* Plant bare-root roses and fruit trees into pots on mild days.

* Continue to feed the garden birds well into late spring; stuff any natural wool, fluffy chicken feathers, or soft dog hair into a little terracotta pot outside as blue tits especially will be looking for the softest of nesting materials.

* Prune established roses, if required, back to visible node-line knuckles or visible buds.

* Plant the last tulip bulbs if any are hanging around.

* Hang lots of golden fairy lights inside, spun through the dried seedheads of alliums and honesty, for sparkle.

* Make lists of wants from plant catalogs— plan summer combinations of annuals and dahlias, cutting out photos and making decoupages.

* Forage silver birch saplings or source a supply of birch and or hazel twigs for plant supports.

* Order snowdrops in the green.

EARLY SPRING

* Pinch out the tips of sweet peas, if they look leggy or once they have four pairs of leaves.

* Begin to water pots of bulbs if the weather is dry.

* Sow tender climbers such as thunbergia and purple bell vine; keep inside on a warm windowsill until the mild nights of late spring (late May in the UK).

* Plant oriental lily bulbs as soon as you buy them.

* Pinch out the growth tips of any hardy annuals in the garden, such as *Cerinthe major*, to encourage bushy growth.

* Tidy and sort sheds and any messy corners of the garden, clutter and fettle!

* Put out cabbage leaves and cut grapefruit halves to lure in slug populations, then go out at night and remove them as they feed, to help curb numbers.

* Protect emerging hostas by smearing petroleum jelly (Vaseline®) around the rims of their pots and by adding seaweed flakes around the spurs of fresh shoots. Cut back old leaves and mulch around ferns in pots; begin to water these if they are in dry shady areas.

OPPOSITE Self-seeded silver birch saplings, foraged while they were dormant in late winter, are pushed into dustbins in groups of five and tied at their tops to create wigwams. Their bushy stems are then twisted from the bottom to the top to create helter skelters, or they can be left as upturned witches' broomsticks.

MID-SPRING

* Plant out sweet peas into their final positions and train them up wigwam supports.

* Deadhead early spring bulbs such as crocus and iris—cut violas and pansies to encourage more flowering, and arrange the flowers in a vase or press them (see page 183).

* Now is the best time to search for molehill soil!

* Continue to water pots of bulbs as tulips come out into full force.

LATE SPRING

* Plant dahlia tubers into 3 liter (5 pint) pots. If they are to be left out at night, cover them with burlap bags in case of late frosts. Guard against slugs—put any plants at risk from nibbling off the ground and on tables.

* Sow the first of the quick-to-grow half-hardy annuals—such as cosmos, tagetes, and panicum.

* Pick the first of the sweet peas and begin to feed them and other pots with seaweed and/or comfrey; feed weekly.

* With the risk of hard frosts now gone, prune back small-leaved salvias halfway, back to fresh buds, or remove dead growth to encourage the basal growth from those such as 'Amistad.' Tender plants such as pelargoniums can be pruned back halfway to encourage fresh growth when they are put back outside. Prune dwarf buddleias by halfway too. Cut back perennial grasses such as *Chasmanthium latifolium* and perennial *Verbena bonariensis* as fresh growth should now be seen at the bases of these perennials.

* Begin to harden off half-hardy annuals you have sown earlier by placing them in the protection of cold frames. Look out for possible self-seeded *Panicum elegans* 'Frosted Explosion' that can be potted up if pricked out when small from between paving cracks.

* Mulch roses in pots now with well-rotted organic manure. Companion plant with *Salvia × jamensis* at their bases to naturally curb blackspot; also begin foliage feeds in the evening weekly.

* Beware of the possibilities of nesting birds in even small gardens—they may make nests in corners where silver birch and canes have been staked, for example, or in evergreens such as yew.

* Monitor lilies for lily beetles, looking for the grubs not just the red adults. Be on constant slug watch, too—inspect under small pots and around growing seedlings and young plants especially.

* Begin to reduce the number of small pots that held the spring show together and focus on the larger pots for planting the annual elements of the summer show within.

* Direct sow annuals such as linaria and borage.

OPPOSITE Don't sow all your summer seeds at once, space them out. Most of mine are sown in the last week of April (mid-spring) so they can quickly be put to grow outside as milder nights begin. Sow seeds thinly; overcrowding is a killer.

EARLY SUMMER

* Begin to mist everything once a week in the evening with either diluted seaweed or comfrey as foliage feeds. Comfrey can be foraged now to ferment as free plant food.

* You can now cut back any herbs that seem to be leggy to healthy buds that are visible on their woody stems, as they have the summer to regrow without risk of frost killing them.

* Save spring bulbs for next year. Either remove the bulbs (if they are to be replanted with summer displays) from pots with their foliage attached and then put them into buckets or wooden trays, placed in a hidden corner of the garden, or allow them to fade, leaving them in the pots but deadhead them.

* Prepare hanging baskets with old sock/wool linings to help them retain water.

* Plant out pot-grown dahlias into their final summer pot positions and arrange annual seedlings such as cosmos and panicum into their groups to grow collectively as trios in their final positions.

* Cut back large leaves of cardoons as they fade to encourage fresh growth.

* Add solar air pumps to container ponds for increased oxygen and to stop mosquitoes.

* Ensure birdbaths are kept clean and topped up.

* Sow the fast bankers—runner beans, sunflowers, and pumpkins. Direct sow cosmos in prepared pots if you haven't sown into seed trays yet. Consider making a second sowing of sweet peas for autumn picking.

* Plant out the tenders that have been waiting for warm nights—*Cobaea scandens* and thunbergia.

* Tie sweet peas and other climbers into their supports, if needed, before flowering makes them heavier.

* Indulge in picking plenty of fresh flowers.

* Continue to pinch out the growth tips of dahlias, cosmos, and other annuals—anything that looks leggy rather than bushy should be pinched! Place strong canes/birch or hazel branches around dahlias before they begin to flower.

* Apply nematodes now on wet days if you have been experiencing very bad slug or vine weevil issues.

MID- TO LATE SUMMER

* Watering and feeding reaches peak levels now—the most stressful and needy time. Be sure to enlist help if you are going away and move small pots into the shade if possible for long weekends when you aren't at home.

* Harvest the faded heads of alliums and honesty to save for winter decor.

* Sow honesty seeds for next year—secure a source of foxglove plug plants for planting for next year's flowers too, or sow the seed. Now is also the time to sow hollyhocks, perennial sweet peas, and kales.

* Cut flowers from annuals and dahlias in abundance—the more you pick the more they'll provide; otherwise you'll have to deadhead them.

ABOVE The essential art of pinching out the growth tips of dahlias, cosmos, and sweet peas, as shown here on a dahlia. Removing the tips creates bushy plants that will produce more flowers (above). A new dahlia bud is firm and shiny like a button (below left) while a deadhead is more pointed and slimy to the touch (below right).

* Deadhead salvias and roses, always to a pair of leaves to encourage more flowers. Say goodbye to sweet peas once they look tired, follow them up with pumpkins, sunflowers, and runner bean seedlings.

* Mulch around the surface of dahlias in pots with either good compost, well-rotted manure, or rotted comfrey.

* Remove old water lily leaves and flowers from container ponds.

* Look out for vine weevils at night by inspecting dahlia flowers and their leaves with a bright light.

EARLY AUTUMN

* Enjoy the abundance—eat outside as much as you can, harvest as much as you can. Take cuttings of salvias and favorite pelargoniums, too, if you can't ensure protection of the parent plants over the coming winter.

* Sow *Cerinthe major*. Source viola plug plants of interesting varieties such as 'Tiger Eye Red.'

* Now is the best time to be planting bought perennials in pots.

MID- TO LATE AUTUMN

* Wait until the summer displays look tired and raggedy before cutting back, then pull out and compost annuals. Use the space to plant the first of the bulbs—honesty, kale, and violas will all want to be planted in their final positions now on top of other bulbs in a

lasagna (see page 90). The sooner the better while the weather is still warm!

* Begin to feed the birds in earnest and ensure bird feeders are cleaned weekly.

* Start to dry out dahlias in their pots in preparation for lifting them into frost-free, cold but not damp places. Lift the tubers from the compost on a dry and sunny day.

* Gather seedheads of panicum to provide natural seeds to feed birds over the winter.

* Transfer pelargoniums and tender plants such as lemon verbena to frost-free places— use dressings of cinnamon powder on top of the compost surface to repel flies if they are to be overwintered indoors on windowsills.

WINTER

* Resist cutting back anything tender in the garden—such as salvias, scented-leaf pelargoniums, and herbs.

* Water overwintering tenders that are inside—namely pelargoniums—sparingly, once every two weeks, but do not allow them to dry out completely. Prune them over, taking off any dying or yellowing leaves.

* Continue to plant autumn bulbs. Gather holly and save any thorny rose prunings to defend against squirrels.

* Plant amaryllis bulbs for indoor flower power.

* Buy snowdrop bulbs in the green, nest them into any unplanted little terracotta pots, and dress them with gathered lawn moss.

Afterword

It is a privilege to know certain plants. Their beauty and spirit bring joy to our lives, and each day, just by looking at them, they lift our mood, which can and does help with our mental health. It's all about giving hope; the razzmatazz of florals is a help and, before you know it, it can get you outside—albeit dressed in jogging bottoms—on what would otherwise have been a blank gray day, planting bulbs instead of pugging on the sofa. And that's a good thing. It means you are out in the fresh air, even if only for ten minutes, because that is better than nothing at all. You are gardening. You are doing something. Well bloody done!

What else is life on this Earth really for? We see in color and we can smell and hear, and we have a brain that allows us to react, adore, and nurture the species that we share this planet with if we choose to. This is what gardening, even on a doorstep, a roof, or a balcony within the busiest and most crowded of cities, allows us to do. You will get visitors as a result, especially pollinators and birds grateful of sanctuary. It creates connections to our natural world, an opportunity to grow beauty. That's why I love pots. We all need to garden for our well-being and for our planet. But don't worry if things fail, just plant them again. Gardening is about daily life—and death. You see every aspect of life within a plant, that is why we need to do it; and the more you garden the more you'll understand your own plot and what thrives there.

No more plastic box balls, please—tear them down! And no more glyphosate because our children and our bees can no longer cope in a world in which it exists. We are running out of time, but that is not a reason to give up hope. Good gardening is power, and even the smallest gardens can add up to collectively change the course of the future.

PREVIOUS Pelargoniums and *Panicum capillare* 'Sparkling Fountain' in very late autumn.

OPPOSITE Every space where plants can be grown without pesticides and herbicides is now precious to both ourselves and our planet's wildlife. Our gardens can be an oasis of life for the greater good of our minds, even if all you have room for is a window box of herbs. It is a privilege to know, and indeed be the conductor, of a garden.

Suppliers and further reading

RECOMMENDED MAIL-ORDER SUPPLIERS

BULBS

Bear Creek Farm
Hudson Valley, NY
www.bearcreekfarm.com
Suppliers of dahlia tubers as well as cut flowers.

Brent & Becky's Bulbs
Gloucester, VA
www.brentandbeckysbulbs.com
All around general bulb specialist for both spring and summer bloomers.

John Scheepers Beauty from Bulbs
Bantam, CT
www.johnscheepers.com
Full range of bulbs for spring, including many of the latest varieties from Holland.

Old House Gardens
Ann Arbor, MI
www.oldhousegardens.com
Specialist in heirloom and vintage bulbs, corms, and tubers.

PLANTS

Almost Eden
Merryville, LA
www.almostedenplants.com
Wide range of perennials including many subtropicals.

Annie's Annuals & Perennials
Richmond, CA
www.anniesannuals.com
Broad range of annuals and perennials, many rare and unusual.

Antique Rose Emporium
Brenham, TX
www.antiqueroseemporium.com
Stocks over 350 antique varieties, including many rustled from old cemeteries and abandoned homesteads.

Avant Gardens
Dartmouth, MA
www.avantgardensne.com
Wide range or perennials with a specialty in succulents.

Broken Arrow Nursery
Hamden, CT
www.brokenarrownursery.com
A collector's nursery filled with an array of trees, shrubs, and herbaceous perennials.

Forestfarm at Pacifica
Williams, OR
www.forestfarm.com
An encyclopedic collection of trees, woody and herbaceous perennials.

Heirloom Roses
Willamette Valley, OR
www.heirloomroses.com
Huge variety of roses all of which are grown on own roots.

High Country Roses
Broomfield, CO
www.highcountryroses.com
Wide selection of own-root roses from old garden roses to modern cultivars.

Plant Delights Nursery at Juniper Level Botanic Gardens
Raleigh, NC
www.plantdelights.com
Focuses on rare and unusual offerings including many North American natives not available elsewhere.

Summersweet Gardens Nursery at Perennial Pleasures
East Hardwick, VT
www.summersweetgardens.com
Specialist in heirloom phlox—also serves a full English afternoon tea during the summer.

SEEDS

Ardelia Farm
Irasburg, VT
www.ardeliafarm.com
Specializes in sweet peas.

Baker Creek Heirloom
Mansfield, MO
www.rareseeds.com
Non-GMO heirloom seeds and modern varieties.

Botanical Interests
Broomfield, CO
www.botanicalinterests.com
Organic, non-GMO flower, herb,
and vegetable seeds.

Diane's Flower Seeds
Ogden, UT
www.dianesseeds.com
Specialist in open-pollinated,
non-GMO heirloom seeds.

Floret Flowers
Skagit Valley, WA
www.floretflowers.com
Family farm specializing
in unique and heirloom flower
seeds.

High Mowing Seeds
Wolcott, VT
www.highmowingseeds.com
Organic seeds.

Renee's Seeds
Boulder, CO
www.reneesgarden.com
Non-GMO seeds for ornamentals
and edibles for home gardeners.

Select Seeds
Union, CT
www.selectseeds.com
Bee-friendly, heirloom seeds
with many rare or unusual
annuals.

GARDEN SUNDRIES
For old dolly tubs and dustbins,
check listings on www.1stdibs.
com, www.etsy.com, and
www.ebay.com.

Arbico Organica
www.arbico-organics.com
Organic fertilizer, compost,
planting mixes, and integrated
pest management products.

Authentic Provence
www.authenticprovence.com
Vintage containers and garden
decor sourced from Europe.

Birdsall & Co.
www.birdsallgarden.com
Containers, birdbaths, fountains,
and outdoor decor.

Campania International
www.campaniainternational.com
Wide range of traditional and
contemporary pots, containers,
planters, and other garden decor.

Gardener's Supply Company
www.gardeners.com
Wide range of garden supplies
including organic products and
peat-free potting soil and seed-
starting mix.

Olde Good Things
www.ogtstore.com
Specialist in reclaimed
architectural items like seating,
statuary, containers, and troughs.

Whichford Pottery
www.whichfordpottery.com
Artisanal pottery available
in the USA through
www.whiteflowerfarm.com.

GARDEN EVENTS & FESTIVALS

Garden Open Days
The Garden Conservancy
www.gardenconservancy.org
Inspired by England's National
Garden Scheme, this annual
program opens private gardens
to visitors from April through
September throughout the USA.

**Philadelphia International
Flower Show**
Philadelphia Horticultural
Society
www.phsonline.org
The USA's largest flower show
and the world's longest-running
horticultural event since 1829.

Trade Secrets
www.tradesecrets.com
Annual spring sale event for
rare plants and garden antiques
whose dates and locations vary
year by year.

INSTAGRAM

Helpful Instagram accounts for container gardening and wildlife, inspiration, and advice:

@annagreenland – Vegetable- and herb-focused grow-your-own advice.

@bethchattogardens – The world-famous dry-tolerant gravel garden that will prove to be even more inspirational in the coming years, with the impact of climate change on our summer temperatures.

@charlie.harpur – Head gardener of the wildlife-friendly pioneering Knepp Estate walled garden.

@clarefostergardens – An encouraging diary of a cottage garden.

@eppinggoodhoney – Artisan beekeepers with huge knowledge and a love of their bees.

@myrealgarden – Ann-Marie Powell—weekly tutorials for gardening in pots and growing advice.

@nate_moss – Incredible photography of butterflies and curator of wildflower lawns at Spencer House in London.

@nigel.dunnett – Pioneering wildlife and low-maintenance garden design, known especially for urban environments.

@pesticideactionnetworkuk – Raising awareness of the harmful effects of chemicals on ourselves and nature.

@thefrontgardeners – Inspirational propagation from a small garden.

FURTHER READING

Bob Flowerdew's Organic Bible:
Successful Gardening the Natural Way, Revised
Bob Flowerdew | Kyle Books, 2012

The Book of Wilding:
A Practical Guide to Rewilding, Big and Small
Isabella Tree | Bloomsbury, 2023

Eat What You Grow: How to Have an Undemanding
Edible Garden That Is Both Beautiful and Productive
Alys Fowler | Kyle Books, 2021

The Garden Jungle: Or, Gardening to Save the Planet
Dave Goulson | Jonathan Cape, 2019

How to Enjoy Your Weeds
Audrey Wynne Hatfied | Sterling, 1971

The Tree in My Garden: Choose One Tree,
Plant It – and Change the World
Kate Bradbury | Dorling Kindersley, 2022

A Year Full of Flowers: Gardening for All Seasons
Sarah Raven | Bloomsbury, 2021

Also by Arthur Parkinson
The Pottery Gardener: Flowers and Hens
at the Emma Bridgewater Factory
The History Press, 2018

The Flower Yard: Growing Flamboyant
Flowers in Containers
Kyle Books, 2020

Chicken Boy:
My Life with Hens
Particular Books, 2023

OPPOSITE Dahlia 'Black Jack' holds court from its tall vantage point in late summer.

Index

First published in the
United States of America in 2024 by
Rizzoli International Publications, Inc.
300 Park Avenue South
New York, NY 10010
www.rizzoliusa.com

Originally published in Great Britain in 2023 as
The Flower Yard: Planting a Paradise—A Year of Pots and Pollinators by Kyle Books, an imprint of Octopus
Publishing Group Limited, Carmelite House,
50 Victoria Embankment, London EC4Y 0DZ

For Octopus
Publishing Director: Judith Hannam
Publisher: Joanna Copestick
Editor: Isabel Jessop
Design: Rachel Cross
Production: Caroline Alberti

For Rizzoli
Publisher: Charles Miers
Editor: Klaus Kirschbaum
Assistant Editor: Emily Ligniti
Managing Editor: Lynn Scrabis

ISBN-13: 978-0-8478-9985-2
Library of Congress Control Number: 2023944558

2024 2025 2026 2027 / 10 9 8 7 6 5 4 3 2 1
Printed and bound in China

Visit us online:
Facebook.com/RizzoliNewYork
Twitter: @Rizzoli_Books
Instagram.com/RizzoliBooks
Pinterest.com/RizzoliBooks
Youtube.com/user/RizzoliNY
Issuu.com/Rizzoli

Page 4 – A red admiral butterfly on a 'Blue Bayou' dahlia.

Pages 6–7 – Picking flowers from the garden creates an essential connection from the garden to the house. A richly perfumed pairing of honeysuckle and *Narcissus poeticus* picked in late spring (left) and an autumn jungle in a vase, including rose 'Mutabilis,' grass *Chasmanthium latifolium*, scabious 'Black Cat,' and dahlias 'Waltzing Mathilda,' 'Verrone's Obsidian,' and 'Totally Tangerine' (right).

Page 208 – Linda, a cream Legbar hen, as a chick.

Endpapers – 'Bocking 14' comfrey and the dahlias 'Bishop of Auckland' and 'Waltzing Mathilda.'

Arthur Parkinson's photography can be found @arthurparkinson_, and his online courses can be found at createacademy.com.

Photographs on pages 1, 12–13, and 193 by Deborah Panes. With thanks to Create Academy for permissions.